IMAGINATIVE HEALING:

Using Imagery For Growth And Change

by

Norman Middleton, MSW

R & E Publishers

This book is sold with the understanding that the subject matter covered herein is of a general nature and does not constitute legal, accounting or other professional advice for any specific individual or situation. Anyone planning to take action in any of the areas that this book describes should, of course, seek professional advice from accountants, lawyers, tax and other advisers, as would be prudent and advisable under their given circumstances.

R&E Publishers
P.O. Box 2008, Saratoga, CA 95070
Tel: (408) 866-6303   Fax: (408) 866-0825

Book Design and Typesetting by elletro Productions

Book Cover by Kaye Quinn

ISBN 1-56875-043-9

Library of Congress Cataloging-in-Publication Data
Middleton, Norman.
    Imaginative healing : using imagery for growth and change / by Norman Middleton.
    p. cm.
    Includes bibliographical references.
    ISBN 1-56875-043-9 (soft) : $11.95
    1. Visualization--Theraputic use. 2. Imagery (Psychology)--Therapeutic use. 3. Self-actualization (Psychology)
    4. Alternative medicine. I. Title.
    BF367.M53   1993
    153.3'2--dc20   93-12861
                                                              CIP

Designed, typeset and totally manufactured in the
United States of America.

DEDICATION

This book is dedicated to Shirley, Norman &
Elizabeth —

the brightest images of all.

ACKNOWLEDGMENTS

This book has its roots in a series of workshops which I presented before the Florida Society for Clinical Social Work over a period of years. I am indebted to the Society for being given the opportunity to present this material and for the support of its officers and members. Special thanks are extended to Catherine Farner, LCSW, who promoted my work so strongly that I finally began to believe in myself.

My own imagery work could not have evolved without a trusted other with whom to journey. By filling that role, my friend and colleague, David Mullen, Ph.D., has made a major contribution to this book. I deeply appreciate his aid.

Recognition is due to Sylvia Ecker for handling secretarial tasks related to the manuscript and to Mary Holmes for research assistance. Heartfelt thanks also go to my wife, Judy, who devoted many hours she really couldn't spare to editing and who remained supportive through the long periods of seclusiveness which preparation of this work demanded.

It is that special group of people which I call my clients who are the heart and soul of this project. They have my appreciation and respect for the courage, humor and trust they have manifested as we journeyed down the rabbit hole together. They are my teachers and I thank them for their lessons.

The author makes grateful acknowledgment to the following for the use of copyrighted material:

HarperCollins Publishers for permission to reprint excerpt from *Peace, Love & Healing* by Bernie S. Siegel, M.D., copyright 1989 by Bernard S. Siegel, published by HarperCollins.

Manuel Komroff for permission to reprint excerpt from *The Brothers Karamazov* by Fyodor Dostoevsky, Translation by Constance Garnett, Published by Penguin Books.

Penguin USA for permission to reprint excerpt from "The Purple Cow" by Gelett Burgess in *Poems That Live Forever*, Published by Doubleday & Company. Also for use of excerpt from *The Natural History of the Mind* by Gordon Rattray Taylor, published by E.P. Dutton.

Sheldon Kopp for permission to reprint excerpt from *Mirror, Mask, and Shadow* by Sheldon Kopp, published by Bantam Books.

INTRODUCTION

THE ENCHANTED THING

In the control room there is an impressive array of panels and switches. Flashing lights and multiple guages give constant reports on the functioning of the various master systems. The room is silent except for the low level buzzing of highly sensitive monitors.

The door opens and an attractive young woman enters. She is initially overwhelmed by the complexity of the technology before her. She begins to scan the identifying labels on the meters. She is looking for a particular one; one that can possibly change her life dramatically.

In a few moments, she has found it. The face of the meter is divided into three sections, one colored green, one yellow and one red. The green section is designated "normal", the yellow section "high" and the red section "extreme." She double checks the label on the meter. It bears the letters ANX. The needle on the dial lies squarely in the red section.

Determinedly, the woman reaches for the knob at the base of the dial. She twists her wrist and finds the knob resistant. She grips harder and applies more strength. The knob begins to turn and the needle starts to move toward the yellow section. As the needle moves, the knob gets easier to turn.

The lady's body language gradually changes to reflect an easing of strain and tension. Soon, she has succeeded in laying the needle to rest in the green section on the dial. She takes a deep breath, exhales completely and smiles.

This woman is a therapy patient practicing the art of private eyeing. The control room is her mental image of her brain, based on the paradigm of a high tech operations center. She is visiting it in her imagination to make needed psychoneuroligical adjustments. She believes that this visualization is having a positive regulating effect on the centers of her brain and nervous system that control her anxiety levels.

Subjectively, the patient feels calmer each time she completes a visit to the central command room of her mind/body system. She believes that the regulating meter she images corresponds to the anxiety governing center of her brain and that her manipulation of the image has a parallel effect on her nervous system. In the interims between visits her anxiety attacks are becoming less frequent and less intense.

Although her understanding of the physiology involved is naive and simplistic, her symptoms do seem to be responding to her imagery. For the first time in her life she is feeling she has some control over her anxiety.

It is difficult to establish with certainty just what imagery can and does do for us physiologically or emotionally but a growing body of research suggests that the benefits may be considerable. Whatever its advantages, many patients and therapists are finding it to be an exciting and enriching modality in which to work.

Since I have been using clinical imagery extensively, I have seldom had to confront issues of boredom or burnout in myself or those I treat. It has an energizing effect that I have not realized with other approaches I have used.

Currently, among providers and recipients of psychotherapy there is a good deal of interest in imagery. Some people are under the impression that it is one of the latest innovations in the field. Nothing could be farther from the truth.

Historically imagery has maintained a consistent, though not always prominent place, in the psychotherapeutic repertoire. Freud used it before switching to free association. It has always been the central technique of Jung's Analytic Psychology. Even behavioral therapists, who earlier in their development declared imagery to be unmeasurable, therefore non-existent and unsuitable for psychological study, have come to employ it.

There is evidence that, throughout much of mankind's life on earth, imagery has been regarded as a source of extraordinary power. This is why it has been incorporated into many forms of religious worship and systems of magic as well as therapy. The Ancients seem to have known what we have recently relearned—

that imagery has value in mind/body healing, problem solving, transcendence, prayer and meditation, life enrichment and personal growth.

This book represents my effort to demonstrate some of the ways in which imagery can be put into practice toward these ends, with emphasis on healing benefits. I have utilized a style of presentation which I believe will convey to the reader the spirit of adventure and the excitement of discovery which is inherent in imagery work.

The overall structure of the book is that of a practice manual rather than a scholarly or theoretical work. The material has evolved from numerous workshops I have presented to clinicians on the subject of imagery and addresses the major questions and points of interest raised at those functions.

Chapter 1 explores the nature of imagery and is followed by a historical perspective on the subject in Chapter 2. Chapter 3 takes a look at the phenomenology of imagery, while Chapter 4 is devoted to the most important adjunct to imagery, relaxation.

Chapters 5 through 14 present a cook book approach, describing ten specific imagery techniques which can be used in a variety of ways. Included are The Inner Child, The Worst Scenario, Symptom Imagery, The Looking Glass Technique, Color Imagery, Dream Imagery, Word Imagery, Shared or Group Imagery, Sexual Opposite Imagery, and The Inner Guide. Verbatim accounts of these procedures and examples based on clinical files are presented to provide the unskilled practitioner and the self-helping layman with sufficient detail to recreate them at the clinic or at home. Personal experiences with these techniques as reported in my own imagery journal are included.

It is, of course, essential that the confidentiality of clients be protected. For this reason case material has been altered sufficiently to make identification of individual parties impossible. Physical characteristics and environmental circumstances have been changed while direct quotations have been rephrased and paraphrased. All of this has been done with the utmost care to preserve the essence of the clinical work.

Some possible uses of imagery beyond the the ten techniques delineated are reviewed in Chapter 15 and special attention is paid to imagery's contribution to various recovery programs. Chapter 16 takes up the controversial issue of imagery's connection with insanity and religious experience. The final chapter is devoted to concluding thoughts on images and imagists.

I believe that this material has special value for therapists who may not have had extensive training in imagery techniques, for clients who are in or have completed a course of psychotherapy, for those in recovery programs and for anyone interested in personal growth and enrichment.

I have been practicing psychotherapy for over twenty-five years and began using imagery about mid-point in my career. In the course of time, I have developed my own style of utilization and that style is adequately illustrated in the examples given. Imagery is a flexible tool that invites individual innovation so readers are welcome to freely adapt the material presented.

In my opinion, imagery is one of the most powerful interventions in all of psychotherapy. I have used it with a broad spectrum of patients excluding those who are acutely psychotic.

I have found it especially productive in the treatment of neuroses, personality disorders, psychophysiological disorders, chronic pain syndromes and sexual dysfunctions. I have used it with individuals, therapy groups, couples and family groups. The case materials I have chosen to demonstrate imagery in action will no doubt convey to the imaginative therapist the variety of applications which are possible.

If you are a psychotherapy patient, please note that the imagery experiences outlined in this book are not intended to replace or to be a substitute for professional help. In my opinion, you will find this or any other self help appproach woefully inadequate if you are trying to cope with a significant emotional or mental illness.

If you are already in therapy, check with your therapist before engaging in any of the imagery exercises suggested in the pages ahead. Make sure they are compatible with the type of therapy you are receiving.

If you are neither a therapist nor a patient and want to experiment with imagery as a tool for enhancing your personal and/or spiritual development, I would suggest that you do so with the assistance of a trusted other if at all possible. This person can present the structured material to you and serve as your sounding board for follow-up discussions. If such help is not available, you will need a recorder for making tapes in your own voice to guide you through the exercises.

With items appearing in the popular press about the use of imagery in treating cancer and other life threatening diseases, I feel compelled to sound the warning that no one should rely on imagery alone to cure *any* physical disease, major or minor. Its benefits appear promising but, in my opinion, it has not been researched long enough or definitively enough for solid conclusions to be drawn.

Nevertheless, imagery can be a helpful adjunct to almost any form of treatment if endorsed by your physician or therapist.

If you do not suffer from any known disorder and develop physical or emotional symptoms after beginning to work with imagery, you should consult a professional right away.

These warnings are not intended to frighten or deter you but, rather, to let you know that imagery is powerful medicine and should be approached with the same caution and respect that you would give a potent prescription drug.

The potential rewards of incorporating imagery into our daily lives far outweigh the few risks. Imagery literally opens up to us a whole new universe of experience with its own landscapes, personages and physics. It makes possible an adventurous journey which can take us to the farthest reaches of time/space and to the limits of our own being.

It was poet Marianne Moore (1944) who called the mind "an enchanted thing" and, indeed, it is. It is a magic carpet, free from the constraints of the physical world. Through imagery, we can exercise the wonderful powers of our mind, harnessing its scarcely tapped energies for healing and growth.

CONTENTS

CHAPTER 1

THE ART OF PRIVATE EYEING

Just about everyone has a favorite fictional detective. Sherlock is mine, hands down.

Granted, the competition is heavy. Miss Marple's sleuthing talents are formidable. The tough guy style of Sam Spade and Phillip Marlowe has a definite appeal. Hercule Poirot and Charlie Chan bring a little humor into their crime solving and Mike Hammer brings a lot of sex into his. By virtue of his sheer genius the great sleuth from Baker Street towers over all of them.

Sherlock Holmes is the creation of Sir Arthur Conan Doyle (1859-1930) who gave him to an appreciative public in fifty-six stories and four novels. The character has found equal favor among movie-goers, turning up as the hero of over one hundred motion pictures.

Holmes, unlike most modern P.I.'s, does not rely on guns and fists to deal with criminals. He is a mental giant who uses deductive reasoning to solve his cases.

Unquestionably Sherlock is an eccentric and non-conforming individual who marches to the beat of a different drum. His most glaring flaw is a penchant for cocaine but that does not prevent him from being an accomplished violinist and a first-rate scientist. He is uncommonly fearless in the face of danger even when it emanates from the personification of evil, his archenemy, Professor Moriarty.

Holmes' adventures can be looked upon as a metaphor for our inner life. Each of us has within us a private eye. It is that part of our personality which is curious, investigative and adept at solving the many puzzles with which life confronts us. It is constantly involved in unearthing clues that reveal what's going on within us and in the world around us.

I identify that part of my personality with Sherlock. That part of me is extraordinarily aware, an observer of details and gifted at reading between the lines.

My Sherlock, like his namesake, has encyclopedic knowledge at his disposal and the courage to grapple with archetypal elements of life. His vision is capable of penetrating to levels of awareness far beyond the ordinary. He is, truly, my own personal private eye or, if you prefer, my mind's eye.

This aspect of each of us finds most of its clues in our imagery. Imagery more than any other phenomenon reveals to us who and what we are at our deepest levels of being.

The private eye within carries on its work whether we are aware of it or not. However, by being aware and consciously utilizing its skills we take advantage of an opportunity to greatly expand our awareness and to enhance our self healing powers.

The First Problem: Definition

Even as I encourage you to use and enjoy the benefits of imagery, I'm not going to tell you what it is. No one is going to do that in a very satisfactory way.

In spite of this, most of us will attest to being able to tune in at will to what seems to be an internal television channel that is continuously transmiting images. Those of us who experience this vividly and take it very much for granted may be surprised to learn that some people deny altogether the existence of imagery.

On the scientific front, there is continuing unresolved debate over whether imagery is just an inferred process involving no essential phenomena or is an actual event occuring at a nonordinary sensory or perceptual level. Some psychologists reject the notion that a visual image is an actual picture in one's head.

Others maintain that images are internal representations, though not duplicates, of that which has been experienced externally and that they play an important role in memory and thinking. I share this particular viewpoint but must take it a step further inasmuch as some of my images are of things and events which I never have and most likely never will encounter in my external environment. They reflect the contents of my own unique imaginings but are no less vivid than those which serve to recreate the things I observe in the external world.

Researchers who accept the existence of images have been busy for years trying to explain what they are. Explanations based on neurobiology have attempted to define imagery in terms of neuroanatomy and physiological processes. They may eventually succeed at telling us *how* we image from the perspective of the operation of our nervous systems.

Explanations of imagery based on cognition have defined it more in terms of its psychodynamic meanings and the psychological motives behind it. This approach may someday yield a more complete understanding of *why* we image.

Neither of these major thrusts in research seems destined to tell us exactly what an image is. Perhaps that is why neither approach, nor even a combination of the two, has thus far achieved widespread acceptance. Leaving the resolution of these problems to research oriented minds, let us proceed to a working definition of imagery for the purpose of private eyeing.

Private eye imaging does not involve our perceptual images, i.e., the images of our external environment which flow into us through our visual/perceptual systems when we are awake and alert. In short, it is not concerned with that which we see or think we see with our eyes.

We like to attach a great deal of reliability to these images. After all, seeing is believing.

The fact is that, though we can come to general agreement with others regarding what we are looking at when we view the same thing, everyone's perceptual images differ a little and sometimes a lot. Essentially none of us see anything exactly the same. Nor do we see anything exactly as it is. This is a fascinating subject in itself but is not our central focus here.

A Working Definition

Imagery, as it is addressed in the following pages, is best defined as "the products of the imagination." This is the stuff we see best with our eyes closed.

It is important to bear in mind that this type of imagery can involve any or all of the sensory mechanisms and is not limited to "pictures." We shall refer to pictorial images as "visualizations," allowing for auditory, olfactory, gustatory, kinesthetic and tactile images as well. Conceivably, a single image might involve all of these sensory modalities at once.

For example, an image of your last rollercoaster ride might include not only the sight of the little cars crawling along the serpentine tracks but also the clickety-clack of the wheels and screams of the riders during the big dips; the smell from the food booths below; the taste of the hot dog you ate just before boarding the ride; the sense of your stomach rising to your mouth when the bottom drops out; and the feel of the cold wind blowing into your face. Our most vivid images tend to be holistic in this fashion.

Most people image predominately in the visual mode but this is by no means universal. I have encountered a few individuals who had little capacity for visualization but who still imaged well on an auditory, kinesthetic or some other level. I have yet to encounter anyone totally incapable of imaging.

These imagined images differ from hallucinations in that they are recognized as emanating from within one's mind whereas an hallucination is erroneously believed to be a perception of something outside of the self system. This is the essential criterion for distinguishing normal imagery from psychotic imagery although there are complexities in doing so which we shall discuss later.

Images can be spontaneously triggered by external events, thought processes, emotions and physiological states. In turn, images can serve to trigger specific behaviors, thoughts, feelings and physiological reactions. This is a characteristic circularity that you will notice as you work with imagery over a period of time.

Spontaneous imagery may be consciously welcomed once it has registered in our awareness. It may be experienced as intrusive and threatening when it is unwanted and/or uncontrollable.

Not all images are spontaneous. All of us can consciously and deliberately generate them by focusing inward and "turning on our imagery channel."

Once they enter into consciousness, images are subject to conscious control and manipulation. We can create them according to our own specifications and make them do whatever we wish.

It is also possible for such control and manipulation to be suspended. When this is done, the images are allowed to evolve in a consciously undirected fashion.

Imagery has been identified as one of the means by which our nervous systems record and store our life experience (Horowitz, 1983). As such, it plays an important role in memory, especially the feeling component of memories. An imaged memory is more likely to evoke emotions than one which is simply verbally recalled.

Imagery is also involved in the process of thinking. As with recall, thinking is not exclusively carried out by utilizing words or images. It is the product of fluid interaction between these modes.

Overcoming Resistance to Imaging

Recent interest in the differentiated functioning of the two hemispheres of the brain has drawn attention to the fact that imaging is more of a right hemispheric activity than left (Ley, 1983). The awareness of brain laterality that many therapy clients have developed with the help of the popular press has proven sometimes advantageous in overcoming resistance to imaging.

Some clients' motivation to work with imagery can be stimulated by informing them that the technique allows them to enjoy the experience of tapping into a relatively undeveloped inner resource, namely the right brain. Since it remains true that most of us tend to rely much too exclusively on the rational, verbal, linear thinking functions of the left brain, many people find an element of excitement and discovery in exercising their right hemisphere's talents.

The laterality issue is also helpful in understanding one of the most common forms of interference when imaging. The left brain, living up to its reputation as "the dominant hemisphere," often intrudes with verbal, logical static that is disruptive to the process. It acts as if envious when the other hemisphere is the center of attention and may delight in raising distracting questions like "where did you leave your car keys?" or "what's for dinner tonight?" as the right brain attempts to do its work.

If imagery work is to be effective, it is important that client and therapist share a belief in its power to inform, guide and heal. More often than not, this is a belief which initially must be transmitted from the therapist to the client.

My clients become quickly aware of my confidence and delight in using imagery. This is helpful in resolving the resistance which many of them have toward the method when it is first introduced.

Most resistance is related to social learning and cerebral dominance. We are culturally inclined to be slaves to the rational, verbal left brain. We are taught from infancy to value and use it. In a scientifically oriented, technological society such as ours, the left brain is sanctified.

The right brain is easily overlooked because it is relatively mute. Despite this, it offers us musical and recognition abilities; non-linear, holistic conceptualizations; and a natural talent for imaging. It is the stuff of which artists and poets are made.

Clients are preconditioned to be embarrassed about performing the irrational act of imaging, much less telling someone about their images. When the therapist further instructs them to get into dialogue with their images, their limits are really pushed.

Their first response to the suggestion that they image something is usually, "I can't do this," or "This is silly."

One of my typical counters to such protests is, "Everyone has an imagination but you probably feel awkward because you haven't been using yours to work on your problems. That's too bad because it is a powerful device. Let's both be patient with you and help you learn how to take advantage of this healing power that you already possess."

To the charge of "silliness," I say, "This is not only silly, it is downright crazy but I think if you will take the risk of being a little crazy you will discover an interesting, new and productive way of working on your problem. After all, you've been wrestling with this problem rationally for some time without very good results. Here's your chance to use another half of your brain which you have mostly ignored."

I tell everyone that the best thing about imagery is that there is no wrong way to do it. There is no expected outcome. We simply work with whatever comes into their mind. If they have difficulties with it, we learn from those difficulties. The only way to muff it is to not even attempt it.

In the end, the vast majority are willing to put their private eye to work. For those who are not willing or just too threatened, there are other treatment approaches.

In the chapters ahead, you will be invited to put your private eye to work. I think you will find that she has all the attributes of Sherlock and more.

If the private eye part of you is relatively unknown to you, don't be deterred. Given a nurturing climate, there's a good chance it will rapidly emerge.

If that part of you has laid dormant for a long while, take heart. You can breathe life back into it. The Sherlock literature bears this out.

The great detective's sleuthing came to a complete halt for a four year period following a battle with Professor Moriarty near a waterfall. Both were believed (by Conan Doyle) to have fallen to their deaths. Both returned to lock horns again as the author responded to an overwhelming popular demand for their resurrection.

Sherlock, as it turns out is practically indestructible. So is your private eye.

The pages ahead offer a variety of assignments on which you can put your private eye to work. They are called secret missions in the sense that they are matters of internal investigation, known only to you. They are forays into the psyche and soul. I will share with you what some others have discovered on such missions via excerpts from my clinical files and personal experience.

But before your private eye sets forth on such a journey, I think it appropriate that you should have some background information. After all, you wouldn't hire a P.I. without knowing something of his history. Besides, I think you will find the history of private eyeing particularly fascinating.

CHAPTER TWO

BISON, REINDEER AND WOMEN

Artistic representations provide our first hard evidence of man's ability to visualize, although it can be assumed that the practice of imaging long preceded the reproduction of imges. Nevertheless, we have been left paintings and sculptures dating back some 30,000 years to assure us that imaging is an ancient practice.

These art finds have been preserved primarily on the walls of caves in France, Spain and other locations. The persons who made them obviously had to have the ability to keep information in their minds' eyes, to formulate a plan transforming it into a picture. How wonderful it is that, thousands of years later, we have no difficulty recognizing their representations.

These early ancestors of ours had to go to considerable trouble to make their paintings and carvings. They were most assuredly not done for decorative purposes as most of them were not placed near the entrance of the caves for easy display but were rendered at remote places, difficult to access and deep within, where the artist had to work by lamplight. We can safely assume that the work was done for some reason more serious than art appreciation and that the subject matter was of central importance to those who labored so hard to create it.

So, what are these images all about? The majority of them are representations of animals. Bison and reindeer are prominent, along with mammoths, horses and an occasional lion, wolf or bear.

There are also a few human figures. Most are exceedingly curious in that they appear to be part man and part animal.

There are also some representations of females, probably motivated by the association of femaleness with fertility. The wonder of the birth process plus the need of the tribe to replenish its numbers in the face of what must have been a high mortality rate no doubt made this a matter of great significance.

The artists themselves were most likely males. That they were indisputably human is attested to by the fact that some of them left outlines of their hands among the paintings as a kind of signature. Like us, our earliest ancestors yearned to be recognized and remembered.

The Mystery of the Cave Paintings

We know that these were people who survived by hunting. The animals depicted in their paintings were primary sources of food to them. They were also sources of considerable danger, given the necessity of facing them head-on with the primitive weapons of the time. They were both feared and revered.

It seems probable that these early humans believed they captured and controlled some of the animals' power by making the paintings. They placed the imaged animals in groupings different from the groupings in which they would have found them in the wild. They juxtaposed one figure upon another and showed some of the beasts succumbing to a well thrust spear. In contrast to reality, their imagery permitted them to completely control these all important sources of both sustenance and danger.

The few human representations seem to be likenesses of very special individuals who had some kind of spiritual or magical connection with the animals and, by implication, had extraordinary power over them. Among these primitive hunters, such persons would have been held in highest esteem.

Since some of the animal paintings show marks of having had spears thrust at them, the hunters may have used them as a means of psyching themselves up for the hunt and as occasional objects for a ritualized form of target practice. Yet, the arduous workmanship that went into the images, their arrangement and their location in the caves all suggest that they were created for something much more profound than mere target practice.

In fact, the cave rooms containing the paintings and etchings may have been early man's equivalent of a sacred chamber, a temple or church. The panorama of animal life depicted and the masterful way in which the images of these all important, yet threatening, creatures were represented must have been awe inspiring to those who crawled through the narrow opening to enter the room.

Here, unlike the outer world where the hunter was barely a match for his prey, man was master. The creatures of the wild were doing his bidding through a spiritual link more powerful than any weapon of the hunt.

No chamber could be more ideal for the most important rite of passage known to these people - the initiation of the young boy into the ranks of the hunters. Here the secret could be revealed to him: that success and survival as a hunter depended on supernatural connections with the deified prey.

The initiate would crawl through a narrow opening every bit as constricting as the birth canal and tumble out into a room where the material universe was refuted and the sacred knowledge which would make him a brave and wise hunter was revealed. The awesome scenes on the wall of that cave room imparted to the boy reverence for the great forces in his life and awareness of the importance of spiritual relations with them. Indoctrinated with this wisdom, he was admitted to the ranks of manhood.

The central point is that all of the images seem to have been endowed with magical qualities. Images were regarded to be of a higher order than the thing itself, perhaps to contain the essence of the thing itself. This concept remained extant for a long time, peaking with the philosophy of Plato.

As noted, a careful examination of the cave paintings uncovers a small set of images which are strange and revealing. Interspersed with all the animal representations are those human figures which are masked to look like animals or which have body parts like animals.

In Up *From Eden*, Ken Wilber (1981), comments on one such etching found in a cave site called Trois Freres in France. This particular figure depicts a man with parts resembling a deer, an owl, a horse and a lion. It has been christened "the sorcerer of Trois Freres" by scholars who have identified it as a representation of a magician. Wilber contends that the artist was projecting in this figure a nature god, a sorcerer, a hunting spirit and himself in an undifferentiated fashion.

This suggests that those who were unusually gifted at creating and reproducing images may have viewed themselves as having special connections to the magical forces of nature. Members of the tribe may have shared these beliefs and have given these individuals a unique status because of their spiritual relationship with the animals they projected on the walls.

It is likely that rituals were developed in which these persons would transform themselves into animal spirits by donning skins, tails, antlers, etc. These were the progenitors of the class which later would be called shamans and priests.

It wasn't long before tools and weapons were being engraved with similar images, perhaps for the magical purpose of enhancing the instruments' efficiency. Caves in Africa attest to the fact that this kind of representation continued for thousands of years. Some of the art work discovered there is nearly as old as that of the European caves but some of it is as young as only 3,000 years. The animal themes continue to dominate in the more recent works.

Imagery After the Caves

With the development of language, reliance on images to communicate became less necessary. Words were substituted for them. Images, which were just once removed from immediate experience, gave way to words, which were twice removed. The emotional content of words was less, making it possible to pass information much more quickly and efficiently and to categorize objects and events more impersonally.

This function of languge took on increasing importance in man's evolution. Language skills and the operations of the left cerebral hemisphere were destined to become dominant forces within the individual and in society.

Nevertheless, in culture after culture, imagery has remained man's closest link to those aspects of being which are most difficult to articulate, such as his place in nature and the universe, the purpose of his existence and his relationship with a Higher Power.

A culture's imagery is chronicled most lucidly in its art works. Fortunately, we have salvaged a rich legacy of such creations dating to the distant past. Affirming the value of imagery in expressing the ineffable, we find many picturizations of deities in addition to men and their deeds.

In the ancient cultures of Summaria and Babylonia sculptures of fertility gods have been found. Egyptian sculptures and paintings abound with representations of their gods. In these cultures, there was an increasing tendency to image gods less as animals and more in human form. Many of the deities preserved the power to transform themselves into animals while others were a mix of animal and human.

In the ancient Grecian and Roman cultures, the human form was especially admired. Not surprisingly, we see in their artworks representations of gods who not only look very human but are choice physical specimens. Interestingly, even in these more advanced cultures, the gods retained a penchant for taking on the forms of animals.

With the evolution of great religious teachers who were also genuine human beings such as Buddha, Jesus and Mohammed, depictions of God in human form became even more prevalent. Michaelangelo's God of the Sistine Chapel is a powerful yet completely human father figure.

In summary, throughout all ages human beings seem to have regarded imagery as the bridge to the divine and, thus, as a source of power. The earliest concept of this power was mainte-nance or restoration of oneness or harmony with the surrounding world of which the individual viewed himself as an integral part.

The Rise of Shamanism

The artist responsible for the sorcerer of Trois Freres perceived himself at once as a hunter, an animal spirit and a magician. He represents a kind of wholeness which was, undoubt-edly, highly valued and held in awe by others. He could claim the world of man and the world of the beasts equally as his own.

Being thus connected with both realms, the sorcerer of Trois Freres has been identified as the first officially recognized shaman. This means that the shamanic tradition is at least 20,000 years old.

Shaman is the correct anthropological term for those who have pejoratively been referred to as witch doctors and medicine men by critical westerners. Shamanism is a system of problem solving and healing that has endured longer than any other. Imagery is its mainstay.

The shaman views illness or injury as the result of loss of one's personal power. Loss of power, in turn, is seen as a disturbance of the spirit. The spirit may have become frightened, depressed or may have abandoned its host altogether.

The first order of business in shamanic healing is to restore the spirit. This takes precedence over preservation of the body. Therefore, a shamanic healing might be deemed successful even if the patient dies. Medicinals and physical manipulations are accepted within the system but are not primary.

The shaman works by entering an altered state of con-sciousness, called the shamanic state of consciousness, in which she experiences extremely vivid imagery. To the shaman, this constitutes a journey to another reality separate from that of space, time, energy and matter.

The purpose of this other worldly venture is to diagnose the patient's disorder of the spirit and to do what is necessary to put things back in order. If the patient's soul has been lost, the shaman must find it in the underworld and return it to the owner. Assistance may come from animal spirits or human guides who protect the shaman during the dangerous journey and also provide helpful information.

Only after restoration of the individual's power, can the source of disease be removed. This is usually accomplished through a variety of rituals and a dramatic, symbolic casting out of the disease entity, often in the form of an insect or piece of tissue which is sucked or pulled from the body.

This enduring healing method is completely reliant on imagery techniques and is of central interest in the history of imagery, particularly its therapeutic application. Western medical scientists have recently begun to reevaluate the healing potential of shamanistic practices for modern man.

For those who wish to pursue a deeper understanding of shamanism, there is a sizeable body of literature on the subject. An especially lucid account can be found in *Imagery in Healing: Shamanism and Modern Medicine* by Jeanne Achterberg (1985).

Imagery, Religion and Medicine

Following shamanic tradition, mystics and holy ones of many faiths have sought transcendent experiences. Like shamans, they have initiated other worldly contact by wandering in the desert, fasting and subjecting themselves to physical pain and deprivation. Practitioners of these behaviors are eventually confronted with vivid images (hallucinations) filled with mystical symbolism.

The power to heal sickness was attributed to the shaman and, later, to the priest/physicians of such cultures as Egypt, Greece and Rome. Healing was as much or more a matter of metaphysics as physics.

The great Renaissance physician, Paracelsus, even though he is known as the father of scientific medicine, continued to declare that imagination and faith have a magical influence on the body. He advocated that medical practitioners should channel divine power, as well as medicines, into their patients.

In the prescientific world, visions had been looked upon as encounters with supernatural forces and those who had them were revered. As man and society came to value rationality and adopted the scientific method as the "right" way to think, the visionary was more and more perceived as being naively superstitious or suffering from mental pathology.

After Paracelsus, those who studied the science of medicine separated themselves from those who practiced the art of healing. This was part of a more general movement by which the Church and Science were going separate ways.

The Church was just as eager for this split as the scientists although historically that is sometimes played down. Scientific findings increasingly were coming into conflict with theological tenets. This severely threatened the fathers of the Church who begrudgingly relinquished knowledge of the material universe to science while proclaiming itself sovereign over all things spiritual.

The end result was that physician and priest became separate entities. The body/brain became the domain of science leaving the mind/soul to religion. Enmity developed between those who healed by faith and those who healed by science. Imagery fell largely into the camp of the faith healers.

There remained one gray area, the no-man's land between faith and medicine—psychology. The psychiatrist, trained in medicine and psychology, retained many functions of the priest and early specialists in the field remained interested in imagery, particularly in its relation to emotional trauma.

Dr. Joseph Breuer, Sigmund Freud's mentor, was using hypnotic imagery to recover repressed memories in his patients when he and young Sigmund first collaborated. Freud incorporated those techniques into his own practice. He encouraged his patients to describe images of past trauma and to relive the associated feelings for cathartic release. He later gave up this procedure in favor of the free association technique though he continued to work intensely with dream images.

The other giant of psychiatry, Carl Jung, who was Freud's contemporary, gave imagery a place of prominence in his treatment approach through the technique he called "active imagination." He instructed his patients to allow images to appear, to observe them and to enter into dialogue with them. His work provides the foundation for most of the modern therapeutic uses of imagery.

If nowhere else, at least in the sector of psychological treatment imagery retained a   position of respectability. This changed, however, when John Watson (1913) published a paper entitled, "Psychology as the Behaviorist Views It."

Watson's branch of psychology, known as behaviorism, sought to make psychology an exact science by dealing only with its observable and quantifiable dimensions. He pronounced unmeasurable phenomena such as thoughts, feelings and images to be unsuitable areas of study, relegating them to the status of non-existence.

Eager to establish parity with the physical and biological scientists and seeing Watson's approach as a way of making psychology a quantifiable, therefore respectable, discipline, the mainstream psychologists were swept away by his theories. No work on imagery appeared in the professional literature for a period of nearly fifty years

Following the rise of behaviorism, imagery techniques were employed only by the few and the obscure. They didn't talk much about it.

The comeback was gradual—here and there an ariticle and, finally, the return of treatment approaches in which imagery played a central role. Notable among these are the works of Leuner (1969), Shorr (1980), Lazarus (1977), Ahsen (1973), Assagioli (1971) and the Samuels (1975).

Recently, imagery has received an additional thrust from excitement over its application in treating life threatening illnesses such as cancer (Simonton, Simonton and Creighton, 1978, and Siegel, 1986). The behaviorists, who once declared imagery anathema, now freely make use of it in such techniques as systematic desensitization (Wolpe, 1969).

From cave walls to houses of worship, from the psychiatrist's couch to modern operating rooms, imagery has survived. It has receded but always has managed to re-emerge as a therapeutic technique. In all cultures and all ages, healers and their patients have turned to it. There is something magical in the nature of imagery that man, so far, has not been able to explain away. This is its fascination and, perhaps, its power.

But, we shall not come closer to understanding this marvel called imagery by observing it from a distance. We must send in our private eye for a closer investigation.

CHAPTER THREE

PURPLE COWS AND OTHER HELPERS

The "imagery channel" within us broadcasts twenty-four hours a day. At any time, we have the option of tuning in to it or not.

All we have to do is close our eyes and ignore all of the other channels which transmit to us. If we are patient, within a few minutes, at most, some kind of visualization will spontaneously appear. It might be a landscape, an object, an animal, a person, a particular place, something abstract or a remembered experience. Any of these entities might be familiar or quite unfamiliar to us.

If we fix our attention on them, the images will begin to develop in some way. They may become brighter or dimmer. They may change in form or context, become animated. They may proceed through a series of actions. They may give way to other images which may or may not seem somehow related to the originals.

Images impress us as having their own energy and purpose. They are directed by sources of which we are unconscious. If we choose to intervene, we can consciously take charge of them and have them do our bidding. Most of the time, we have the power to turn them off at will.

Another way we can use our "imagery channel" is to project on it images of our own choosing as when we entertain romantic or sexual fantasies. These we can manipulate in any way we like or, having put them on the screen, we can refrain from consciously

17

controlling them and let them do what they will.

Sometimes, the channel flips on without our bidding and images intrude on our consciousness. Depending on their nature, they may or may not be welcome. They may have been evoked by either an external or internal triggering mechanism. More often than not, we are unaware of what that trigger is.

Since images are closely tied to our emotions, they are usually accompanied by feeling states. Daydreamers spend a lot of time with their images because of the pleasant feelings they evoke. At the opposite pole, a person who is severely disturbed emotionally may be reluctant to close her eyes because she dreads the frightening images which may appear and the horrible feelings which come with them.

The Therapeutic Use of Imagery

When we put imagery to work therapeutically, we are using it as a special language. When we visit a foreign land, we have much more access to the culture if we speak the language. We can understand things more clearly, go places more easily and interact more richly with the environment.

The language of imagery allows us to have certain kinds of experience which our ordinary (verbal, rationally structured) language does not. For example, imagery gives us access to certain types of information.

This is easily illustrated if you will allow yourself to access the year in which Columbus discovered America. Consider for a moment the process you went through to come up with 1492.

Chances are you quickly referred to a kind of mental index of information and found it there as a fact on file. Perhaps you recited to yourself a little rhyme you learned as a child.

In contrast, allow yourself to access the number of windows in your living room. Most likely, the process you went through to get that information was very different, involving referral to an image of your living room and counting the windows.

Our stored information is packaged in words and images. We cannot assign more importance to one modality than the other.

Since it took us a number of years to access our language, it stands to reason that information relating to the predominately pre-verbal period of our lives (infancy and early childhood) was stored more in the imagery mode than the lexical mode. Therefore, one of the ways we can use imagery in therapy is to help clients retrieve important early life memories.

This can be accomplished by starting with a feeling that is

rooted in the client's past but to which no conscious memories are attached. Through uncensored imaging while in touch with that feeling, the unconscious may gradually or suddenly reconstruct for the client partial or complete recall of some past event.

The same procedure can be followed by starting with a partial or fleeting image which the client recognizes as related to some forgotten experience and allowing a free association of other images to evolve around it. Like pieces of a picture puzzle, the images may produce a mosaic of an early life event.

The Case of the Threatening Hands

To illustrate, allow me to introduce you to a former client of mine named Jerry. He was a thirty-one year old banker who suffered from anxiety attacks. He noticed that his anxiety intensified when he had to carry out business or social transactions with men older than himself.

Although he remembered very little of his father, who died when Jerry was seven, his mother told him that he and his dad had enjoyed a close relationship. She did not remarry after the father's death, so Jerry grew up with no prominent masculine person in his life but he got along well with his male peers and was unusually well behaved around male authority figures.

At the beginning of therapy, I taught Jerry how to use imagery as a method of relaxation. He was soon becoming quite relaxed as he visualized walking along his favorite beach on a lazy, summer day. His images were vivid and his attention on them well focused but they were at some point usually disrupted by the intrusive image of a disembodied pair of hands which produced instant anxiety.

Although he was extremely frightened to do so, I encouraged Jerry to confront those hands by giving them his full awareness instead of trying to make them disappear as he usually did. By degrees he did this, finally drawing close to them in his imagination. To his shock and horror, the hands grabbed hold of him and began beating him viciously.

That imagery released the memory of an incident which occurred when the client was about five years old. He had run up to his father who was seated in a chair reading a newspaper and had flung himself in his lap. Father became suddenly enraged, hurling Jerry to the sofa and hitting him hard with his fists.

Following this recall, Jerry remembered other instances of being brutalized by his father. He confronted his mother with these memories and she became extremely agitated but finally acknowledged their validity.

She informed Jerry that his father had been an alcoholic, given to aggressive rages when drinking. He had beaten both of them many times and died in an automobile accident while driving under the influence.

In the ensuing years, Jerry's mom noted that her little boy didn't seem to remember the bad times and decided she would be doing him a favor by painting his father in a positive light. Thenceforth, she told him only favorable things about their life as a family, most of which was pure fabrication.

Jerry had repressed the painful events connected with his father but the anxious feelings attendant to them remained with him throughout his adolescence and adulthood. His cautiously good behavior around male authority figures in his youth was based on an underlying fear of attack. His anxiety was later transferred to any older male with whom he had to interact.

Imagery brought the dynamics of his problem right to the surface and enabled us to explore the emotional conflicts originating in his relationship with both mother and father. In the course of treatment, Jerry's condition improved.

Imagery and the Body

Imagery is also the language of access to a significant branch of the human nervous system. We have a central nervous system composed of the brain and spinal cord and a peripheral nervous system made up of the nerves projecting from the central system. The peripheral system, in turn, is divided into the somatic system and the autonomic system.

The somatic nervous system which controls the action of our muscles is accessed by sending a conscious message from the brain to the muscle groupings involved in specific movements. You can experience this action simply by raising your hand and observing the process by which that action is accomplished. You instruct the hand to go up and it obeys immediately.

The autonomic nervous system, on the other hand, is responsible for automatically controlling the function of our glands and structures like our lungs, heart, blood vessels and the pupils of our eyes. This system is unusually responsive to imagery.

By and large, the autonomic nervous system is not responsive to conscious, verbal commands as is the somatic system. I can tell my pulse rate to increase but it is unlikely to obey that order. On the other hand, I can spend some time imaging something very frightening or disturbing and there is a very good chance my pulse rate will increase.

It is a truly remarkable phenomenon that a basic physiological function can be altered solely by imagination. The therapeutic implication of this is that we can significantly influence basic bodily functions and correct malfunctions.

To fully appreciate this, we need to keep in mind that the autonomic system is divided into two sub-systems: the sympathetic and parasympathetic, each acting in opposition to the other to maintain bodily homeostasis. When the need arises, the sympathetic system serves to step up bodily functions, increase heart rate, dilate pupils and to redirect blood supply from the intestines to the brain and muscles. The parasympathetic system carries out reverse operations once the call to action has passed.

The ability to control the activities of these two systems could aid significantly in the prevention and treatment of many physical diseases, emotional disorders and stress reactions. There is growing evidence that imagery may be the key to establishing such control.

Though there is still much investigative work to be done on the subject, imagery appears to be the language of access to the human immune system. This awareness has led to the development of a new field of scientific investigation called psychoneuroimmunology.

It is the function of the immune system to protect the body from invading organisms and to participate in healing once damage has been incurred. There are many complex biochemical processes involved in the operations of this system which mounting evidence shows can be influenced by the imagination.

Positive images of the immune system's functions at work seem to enhance their effectiveness. For example, images of anti-cancer cells massacring their foes may promote adjunctive healing along with traditional medical approaches. Imagery of medicine or other forms of treatment reducing inflammation, killing invasive organisms or reviving damaged tissues may increase the potency of the medicine. These and other medical uses of imagery will be discussed more fully in Chapter 16.

Transcendence Through Imagery

In addition to its clinical applications, imagery retains its place as the language of access to transcendent experience. Along with prayer and meditation, it is one of the ways through which individuals have sought and continue to seek connection with a Higher Power. It has been used in the seeking of enlightenment, communion with God, divine revelation and other transpersonal phenomena.

In the light of present knowledge, the validity of these experiences cannot be established. Perhaps, it will never be possible to do so from a rational, scientific perspective.

Many of those who use imagery extensively, like myself, at times have a feeling of being freed from the bonds of the universe of space, time, energy and matter. Imagery enables us to visit realms of experience which seem entirely real but which are not subject to the same laws of physics as the material universe.

These realms may be an example of what Carlos Castenada's (1971) Yaqui medicine man, don Juan, called a "separate reality. His way of knowledge allows inner experience to be treated as no less of a reality than experience of the outer world.

One thing is certain. If you involve yourself deeply in imagery, whether as a therapist, patient or interested layman, you may have to rethink your ideas about the nature of reality and sanity.

The process of therapeutic imaging would be viewed by a large segment of society as totally irrational behavior. It entails treating our images like real entities—calling them by name, treating them respectfully and carrying on dialogues with them.

The average person observing a therapy session in which imagery is being utilized would be likely to judge both the therapist and patient to be around the twist. In a later chapter, we shall explore the sanity issue in relation to imagery in depth.

One of the basic principles of imagery work is that, since all of our images originate within us, they are primarily projections of our selves and our experiences. Though I may suggest a particular image to a patient, what appears is not my image but his. He will visualize it in his own idiosyncratic way. I cannot determine how the patient will structure that image nor what he will do with it once it takes form. It is inescapably a reflection of who he is.

The image, being a manifestation of some aspect of the self, provides the patient with an opportunity to confront that part of herself. It can be manipulated, it can be talked to, it can be listened to, it can be put in touch with other parts of the self. The options are numerous.

An image can be worked with, no matter what its content. These right cerebral hemisphere productions do not comply with the left hemispehre's demand for logical relatedness or rational consistency, leading Lefty to promptly call for the disregard and/ or dismissal of them. The therapist corrects for this by exhorting the patient to refrain from censorship and to be accepting and appreciative of any image that appears to her.

We have all taken delight in Gelett Burgess' (1965) little

rhyme that states:

> I never saw a Purple Cow;
> I never hope to see One...

However, in imagery purple cows, orange horses and pink lions are commonplace. Moreover, we can benefit just as much from an encounter with one of these as with an archetypal wise man.

As we look now at specific applications of imagery be prepared to see some things you never hoped to see and to learn from them. Be aware that your helpers may be a strange lot: animals, objects, exotic persons, deities - even purple cows.

CHAPTER FOUR

QUIETING THE DRUNKEN MONKEY

In *What To Do Till the Messiah Comes*, Bernard Gunther (1971) metaphorically refers to the mind as a drunken monkey in the throes of reacting to a scorpion bite. Truly, the mind of the average, late Twentieth Century American is like a busy switchboard, deluged with information originating within its own call station as well as that coming from the outside world. In regard to imaging, this renders the instrument essential to the task the chief obstacle to carrying it out.

We are raised with a kind of ethic which says, "Keep your eyes open, stay on your toes and you'll know what's happening." In other cultures, predominately Eastern, the ethic is quite the opposite—"If you really want to see what's happening, relax and close your eyes."

Unlike our Eastern brothers, we are not brought up to place much value on quiet, contemplation or meditation. Many of us have begun to recognize that these arts can contribute much to health, wholeness and inner peace but there are many more who know little or nothing about them.

Relaxation and Imagery

Many people in today's world seldom, if ever, relax. Many don't have the foggiest notion of how to relax. One of my clients endeared herself to me forever by saying, "Trying to relax makes me tense."

Relaxation has healing benefits and, fortunately, can be learned. Since it is difficult to image with a cluttered mind and stressed out body, it is important to relax the mind/body system before carrying out any mission involving therapeutic imagery.

Relaxation enhances imagery and vice versa. Images visualized in a relaxed state are more vivid and the entire experience carries more feeling of the imaged events being real and immediate. Since relaxation also heightens suggestibility, all of the imaged sights, sounds, tastes, smells, feelings and actions become the client's reality of the moment as the external environment is excluded from his awareness.

I begin every therapeutic imagery session with a brief relaxation procedure. If a client comes to me already knowing a method, I encourage him to use it as a prelude to our imagery work. If the client does not know such a procedure, I will teach one.

The method by which the client relaxes is not crucial. Yoga breathing, progressive relaxation and hypnotic trance are all acceptable modalities.

It is best to practice imagery away from interruptions and noise. Ideally the office of an imagery therapist is quiet and the atmosphere is unhurried. A comfortable couch or chair for reclining is also an asset but none of these trappings are indispensable if the therapist is patient, calm and self assured.

I was able to prove that point a while back when a nearby hospital began constructing a parking garage across the street from my office. For several days (it seemed like months) the sound of piledrivers filled our ears with incessant pounding. There was no way to ignore it during relaxation procedures.

My preferred approach to relaxation is basically a trance induction. I begin by having the client get comfortably situated in a recliner, take three deep breaths and allow the eyes to close on the third exhale. Then, I suggest that he entertain an image of tension in the form of a vapor flowing out the tips of the fingers and tips of the toes, followed by an image of all the muscles of the body going loose and limp. The next step is for the client to calmly and quietly leave the immediate environment behind as he begins to journey deeper and deeper within.

While the construction was going on, I simply suggested that the pounding be experienced like the beat of a drum and that, with each beat, the client would find himself going deeper and deeper into the trance state. It worked quite well.

No matter what approach is being used, it is proper procedure to give the client some repetitive suggestions while the relaxation is unfolding. It helps to remind him that any distracting thoughts can be allowed to simply pass by without commanding any attention and that there need be no concern about performance. In regard to the latter, I usually say something like, "There's nothing you have to do except let go and allow whatever happens to happen."

Questions are often raised regarding how deeply relaxed or in trance the client should be before beginning imagery. From my experience, many clients image quite well from a state of very light trance. There is nothing to indicate that a deep trance state is required.

In most cases, a sufficient induction of relaxation can be completed in about ten minutes or less. Remember that working with images in itself is a deepening technique and that the client will probably be going deeper as the session progresses.

Deepening suggestions can also be implanted during the imagery work. For example, if a client is involved with an image of his anxiety symptom in the form of a little red wagon and it becomes desirable for him to go deeper, I might suggest that he visualize the wagon beginning to roll down a hill in slow motion and have him go after it, one step at a time, going deeper and deeper into a trance with each step.

Relaxation Versus Hypnosis

The relaxation versus hypnosis question comes up frequently in training sessions for therapists who want to practice imagery. It is an issue with some clients as well. Is the imaging client just relaxed or is she hypnotized?

It is a difficult issue to clarify. Conceivably, deep relaxation, hypnosis and meditation are all manifestations of the same phenomenon. Each represents an altered state of consciousness in which the person's attention is focused very differently than it is during her ordinary state of conscious awareness. The term "hypnosis" sparks a much more emotional response in people than does relaxation or meditation, although the final state to which each one leads is equally mysterious.

Hypnosis seems never to have been able to escape its roots which have been intertwined with charlantanism. After all, it was the famous physician of Vienna, Franz Mesmer, who first promoted its use in the "cure" of a variety of illnesses. He explained the effects of hypnotic suggestibility as the products of a force he called "animal magnetism."

Mesmer gained notoriety by debunking the "miracle" cures of a German priest, Father Gassner, who had attracted much attention all over Europe. Before an ecclesiastical commission, Mesmer demonstrated that he could effect cures similar to those brought about by Gassner but based on scientific rather than supernatural principles. His performance, which many found astounding, was an application of hypnosis.

Caught in the limelight, Mesmer set up a practice in Paris and elaborated on his theory which postulated that illness was the result of insufficient magnetic fluid in the body. He devised tubs on the order of storage batteries around which his patients sat holding on to spoke-like handles projecting from their center. Through this process they supposedly absorbed the magnetic fluid being generated within the tubs.

With a grand display of showmanship, Mesmer would occasionally sweep into the treatment room and touch the patients with a wand or his fingers. The entire setting was conducive to trance induction and Mesmer's magic touch was a powerful suggestion for healing.

Mesmer was later discredited by a tribunal appointed by King Louis XVI composed of prominent French scientists and the American ambassador to France, Benjamin Franklin. Mesmerism, the precursor of hypnotism was renounced and the evidence of it having actually produced some cures was discounted. The proverbial baby was thrown out with the bathwater.

In 1843, James Braid, the English surgeon who performed operations on people in trance states without benefit of anesthesia, gave mesmerism a new name, hypnotism, and it began to regain respectibility. It was and still is not completely understood.

Freud's interest in the use of clinical hypnosis was sparked by his teacher, Bernheim and his close colleague, Joseph Breuer. Even though he abandoned the technique, it continued to be a tool utilized with some frequency in the field of psychiatry.

In recent years, there has been a grand resurgence of interest in clinical hypnosis thanks in great part to the work of Milton H. Erickson (1980). He projected the viewpoint that trance states are a common and natural phenomenon in everyone's life and that they could be induced permissively with little fanfare. His approach is ideal for clinical work in general and imagery work in particular.

Combining Hypnosis and Imagery

As far as I'm concerned, when my clients are imaging intensely, they are hypnotized. Imagery and hypnosis flow together so naturally and spontaneously that I do not place much emphasis on the hypnotic aspect when preparing people for imagery work.

I usually say something like, "When people image intently they often enter a state of hypnotic trance. Does that possibility present you with any questions or concerns?" If their response is affirmative, we address those issues before proceeding.

Most clients subjectively describe their imaging state as a non-ordinary state of consciousness. The astute therapist will keep in mind that it is a state of heightened suggestibility and will implant suggestions helpful to the client as the imagery unfolds.

I include here my version of an induction which can be used verbatim or with modifications. If you have no partner with whom to do your imagery work you can make an audio tape of it using your own voice. This is usually quite effective.

Where there are a series of dots (...) be sure to pause significantly. An induction should never come across as rushed.

Begin by taking a deep breath and exhaling slowly through your mouth...Notice the relaxation in your chest and abdomen as you breathe out...Take a second deep breath and exhale slowly...Feel the relaxation...Now, take a third deep breath and, this time, as you exhale, allow your eyes to close...With your eyes comfortably closed, just breathe normally...Allow any tension anywhere in your body to flow out of you...Visualize it as a vapor that is right this minute flowing out the tips of your fingers and the tips of your toes...Feel your muscles going loose and limp as the tension leaves your body...

You've begun a process of physical relaxation that will continue on its own as long as you do not intefere with it...Just let go and allow it to continue...There is nothing you have to do...No effort of any kind is required of you...Just let what happens happen...

While you're becoming more and more deeply relaxed, allow your conscious mind to drift away from your immediate surroundings...You're on a journey deep inside yourself...Everything outside just fades away as you feel yourself moving deeper and deeper inside...It's like being on an escalator that's taking you slowly and gently to deeper and deeper levels of yourself...The ride makes you feel far away, detached and drowsy...The deeper you go, the more calm and peaceful you feel...

You may have already noticed that your arms and legs feel heavy...The muscles in them have relaxed to such a degree that it feels like it would take a great effort to move an arm or a leg and it's nice to know that you don't have to...You can just continue this pleasant ride to deeper and deeper levels within...Time is slowing down, giving you lots of time to go as deep as you wish...

At the end of your journey, you'll be encountering some images which are there to help you learn, explore and heal...It's good to know that, in your relaxed state, all the systems of your body are functioning smoothly and efficiently...Your body requires none of your attention at all...So, you can be pure mind, ready to receive helpful images and suggestions which can be used in whatever way is best for you...You can go even deeper to get maximum benefit from this experience...You can just float down the rest of the way, like a feather in the breeze...You're floating down...down...down.

This much of an induction usually takes the client deep enough to begin imaging. Remember that the imagery itself may spontaneously bring about further deepening or can be used as a vehicle for giving deepening suggestions.

The drunken monkey has been quieted. From this point on you are working with your client's or your own private eye or inner observer. The journey on which you are about to embark is a safari into the densest regions of your inner world, a truly secret mission.

CHAPTER FIVE

THE KID

A good place to begin healing imaging is at the beginning. That means our childhood experience.

Who among us does not have mixed feelings about that time of life? Sometimes we long for the innocence, enchantment and protectedness we knew then. Sometimes we loathe the domination, embarrassment and growth pains we suffered.

In the animal kingdom, mankind is unique in its protracted period of dependency and slow attainment of self sufficiency. We are children for a very long time. No matter how loving and secure our environment, we have all known the fear associated with the feeling of helplessness. It is experienced by every child.

What Makes Childhood Painful?

At some point in our development, each of us had to face that moment when the caretaker(s) wasn't there right when we needed him or her. In that instant, we realized in terror that we could be abandoned and knew the existential anxiety associated with dependency. Residuals of that initial anxiety remain with us throughout life.

In our infantile helpless state we naturally look up to the caretakers on whom our very existence depends. From our vantage point of smallness and insignificance, we initially perceive them as magical, wondrous beings. Throughout infancy and early childhood, we view them as having unlimited knowledge and power. We want their total attention and unfailing love.

No one gets 100% unconditional love from the caretakers and that is not a tragedy. It is what nature has ordained for us. If we did get it, we might never choose to separate from those on whom we depend.

Luckily, most of us get enough unconditional love to enable us to conclude that we are worthwhile and important, even while we are still little and helpless. Recognizing that our all-knowing caretakers regard us highly, we tell ourselves that we must be pretty significant and begin to develop self esteem.

This process hinges on our being cared for physically, nurtured emotionally and thereby developing a perception of the outer world as a relatively safe and friendly place. Those who feel a yearning to return to their childhood years are undoubtedly longing to recapture that sense of belonging and protectedness.

In the worst childhood scenarios, there is no unconditional love at all and/or there is physical and mental brutalization. This is a nightmare to which no one wishes to return. At best, it represents profound parental psychopathology. Otherwise, it is the ultimate betrayal of the human soul.

Those of us who do not experience this extreme still come to know hurt, rejection, disappointment and rage when we are children. Such feelings contribute to the existential pain that we associate with our childhood state.

Over a period of many years, as we mature we fight ever harder to establish an individualized identity. In doing so, we feel pitted against those upon whom we are most dependent and whom we most love.

If we do not subdue those on whom we depend, we are apt to feel a loss of personhood. If we do subdue them, we are apt to feel abandoned. There is no escape from either agony. Resolving this dilemma is the rite of passage into adulthood.

The Nature of the Inner Child

Growing up does not mean shucking off the thoughts, feelings, wishes and attitudes that we had as children. All of that stays with us as an aspect of our personality.

We do not grow out of childhood; we grow up around it. Therefore, a part of us is and ever shall be the little child we were. If we are willing to observe ourselves, we can see this inner child in action many times a day.

Eric Berne (1972) identified this aspect of the total personality as the Child Ego State. He defined an ego state as "a coherent system of thought and feeling manifested by corresponding patterns of behavior."

When we are functioning in our Child Ego State, we are thinking, feeling and acting as we did when we were very young. When we are not functioning in that particular ego state, it is suppressed within us, potentially available for enactment at any time.

The Inner Child, then, is a real, verifiable and holistically valuable part of us. It is a more feeling than thinking part of us because it originated during that period of development when we were beings more capable of feeling than thinking. It is the repository of our most soaring joy and our most exquisite pain.

It is this feature which leads many individuals to develop defenses which insulate them from their Inner Child. When they draw near to that part of themselves they feel first the pain which seems to rise to the top and obscure other, better feelings.

Fearing that the pain will be overwhelming they make an effort to avoid it and, over a period of time, these persons develop a psychological encasement which keeps the kid covered up from outside awareness and insulated from inner experience. The child is, in effect, buried alive and its pain, though obscured, is intensified.

Those of us who do not seek to avoid our Inner Child altogether may, nevertheless, deny certain facets of it. We may accept only the happy, playful kid and reject the sad one. We may like the excited, curious child but give no freedom of expression to the angry one.

It is logical to want to evade discomforting emotions. However, we need to recognize that, though we may give them the slip time and again, this will not make them go away. Feelings defy resolution except through conscious processing. Our avoiding, denying defenses serve only to leave us unconsciously stuck with our dreaded feeling states.

A basic paradox is involved. Make up your mind that, no matter what, you must not think about a specific thing and you will necessarily end up thinking about it more than ever. Avoidance equals stuckness.

Many people are stuck with toxic, even debilitating, feelings related to their growing up experience. Often, they take the intellectual position that the Inner Child is weak, crazy or dangerous. Their left cerebral hemispheres are tyrannical dictators who legislate the Kid out of existence with cold, rational, controlled logic. Such individuals are ideal candidates for an imagery encounter with their Child Ego State.

One does not have to have a problem in order to benefit from encounters with the Kid. The Child can provide us with important, ongoing information about our inner emotional climate. It piques our curiosity about things, knows how to play, is affectionate and loving, enjoys sex and is very creative. Without full interplay with the Kid, we are not complete persons.

Numerous therapeutic goals can be realized by having a client image her Inner Child. It is often the first imagery exercise I do with an office client but this is not exclusively so.

There is no hierarchy of techniques in imagery work so one can begin with any task. They are all equally potent. Depending on what the client needs, some or all of the tasks presented in this book may be appropriate during the course of treatment. Many, like this one, you may want the client to repeat a number of times.

Many clients intuitively recognize their need to connect with their Inner Child and readily become absorbed in the task. Most of those who have difficulty with it easily grasp the significance of their difficulty in terms of their avoidance defenses and can set to work on demobilizing them.

The Case of the Little Bowman

Invariably, meeting the Kid turns out to be an emotive experience, much to the surprise of patients who rely heavily on intellectualization. This is best illustrated by a clinical example in which the private eye makes some startling discoveries through observation of and interaction with the Innner Child image.

Hank was thirty-one years old and depressed when he came to me for therapy. He had been working as a stockbroker for about a year but was not generating much business. Prior to that, he held a managerial position with a retail chain but left because there was no room for advancement.

Hank had been married to Aleen for five years and they had a three and a half year old child. Their intimacy level progressively deteriorated after the birth of the child and he began having erection difficulties about two years prior to consulting me. For the last three months, he had been having sex with another woman and was functioning satisfactorily with her but felt guilty about his infidelity.

Though he knew he was depressed, Hank wasn't actually feeling much of anything. He viewed himself as a failure in all walks of life but went through his daily routines mechanically and quietly. He neither laughed nor cried nor derived much enjoyment from anything he did. He was completely cut off from his Inner Child.

In presenting historical data, Hank reported that his father was a judge, highly intellectual, haughty and aloof from the family. He mostly ignored Hank who was passive and average in just about every way. He showed more interest in Hank's older brother, Scott, who had been an aggressive, hard driving and competitive child and was now a successful attorney.

Hank was clearly his mother's favorite. She confided in him about her deep resentment toward his father, often literally crying on his shoulder.

She regularly referred to Hank's father as "his honor" in a demeaning fashion. She seemed to delight in going out of her way to embarrass the judge who was sensitive about his social image. She often drank too much at gatherings and said inappropriate, negative things about him in the presence of others.

During one of the periods of extreme marital conflict, mother left the gas stove on in the kitchen and an explosion resulted. She was alone in the house at the time but was only singed. Hank had always felt she had done it on purpose to cause his father public embarrassment.

In the course of reviewing his relationship with his parents, the client acknowledged having extremely ambivalent feelings toward his mother. She was not critical of his performance as was his father but he felt exploited by her leaning on him emotionally and was angered by her vicious behavioral ploys to get back at her husband.

In regard to father, Hank hated his pompous manner and distant, disapproving attitude but he sometimes felt sorry for him as he watched him trying ineffectively to control his mother's acting-out of her hostility. He thought his situation with his father, who often referred to himself as a "self made man," might have something to do with his feeling that he would never be a successful person like the judge.

Hank realized that, sometime early in his development, he had decided to be passive and unobtrusive because he did not want to be like his father. He also recognized early on that he had learned to discount and suppress his most intense feelings because no one in his family wanted to be bothered with his feelings. Dad was too uninvolved to care and mother was concerned only with dealing with her own feeling states. Hank's process of disconnecting with his Child had begun when he was very young and, at the time we worked together, had become second nature to him.

At our second meeting, I enthusiastically began to talk with Hank about the use of imagery techniques to help resolve his depression and improve his self esteem. He said it sounded "hokey" to him but he would go along with anything which would help him to "feel like a human being" again.

Notice how well his terminology describes the impact of being alienated from one's Inner Child. It takes away one's humanity and reduces one to the functioning of a robot.

In our third session, as we began our imagery exercise, Hank did not know what I would ask him to image. We went through a relaxation procedure which was moderately successful and, then, it was time for me to introduce the image. The following is a verbatim excerpt from our tape recorded session. The designations T (therapist) and P (patient) are used to denote the speaker.

> T: In a moment, I'm going to ask you to work with a specific image. Remember, we can learn something valuable from anything that comes to you, so don't get caught up in trying to create a "perfect" image. Even if you have difficulty with it, that, too, is useful information. Also, don't censor. Accept whatever appears.
> P: O.K.
> T: Very well. I'd like you to get in touch with an image of you as a child. When you have that image, please describe it out loud to me.

(Hank did not say anything for about twenty seconds. There was lots of eye movement beneath his closed lids, assuring me that he was visualizing.)

> P: I see it.

(Again, notice his terminology. He depersonalizes the Child by calling him "it.")

> T: Please tell me in as much detail as possible what you see.
> P: It's me. I'm probably nine years old... I'm standing out in the yard holding the bow from my little archery set... I"m standing in profile. I can only see my right side.
> T: O.K. Stay with your image, now. What else can you tell me about the kid?
> P: Well, my hair's cut real short - like a G.I. I'm wearing a T-shirt and short pants.
> T: What about colors? Are you aware of colors?
> P: The shirt's yellow and the pants are brown... I'm standing on grass - green grass.
> T: Can you see your face?
> P: I can see the side that's turned to me.
> T: How would you describe your expression?
> P: Well, there's a little smile there. In some ways it reminds me of a little, old man's face. Too serious for a child.
> T: What are your hands doing?
> P: I only see the right one. It's holding the bow.
> T: And your feet?
> P: I'm barefoot. I'm standing sort of at attention with my feet

together.

(At this point, I have elicited enough detail from Hank to ensure that he is visualizing fairly vividly. If there were some doubt, I would continue to press for description.)

> T: O.K. Sounds like your image is pretty complete. Check on your feelings as you continue to visualize. What are you feeling?

(As Hank allows his visualization to intensify and brings feelings about it into focus, the Child begins to take on the attributes of a real person.)

> P: (Immediately) Nothing. (Pause) I can't help feeling a little sorry for him. He just doesn't look like a kid should look. There's no...There's nothing carefree about him.
> T: That's you.
> P: Yeah. (Soberly) I guess I was this way even when I was little.
> T: Are you staying with your image?
> P: Mmmmm.
> T: O.K. If you're willing, why don't you try to get little Hank to face you?
> (Silence for ten seconds)
> T: Are you getting him turned?
> P: This is really strange. I know I should be able to do this. But I tell him to turn and he just won't do it.

(At this juncture, I had no idea why the image was fixed in profile but did not wish to make an issue of it on the grounds that it might put Hank and the Child in opposition to each other.)

> T: Well, let's just accept him as he is. Can you give me some detail about the background to your image?
> P: It's the back yard of the house I grew up in. It's fairly large. There are a couple of oaks - one I like to climb a lot. There's a shed where yard tools are kept. Right now I'm thinking I spent a lot of time alone in that yard. I don't think I had many friends.
> T: Does the image connect with any specific event in your early life?
> P: No... I mean, I remember getting the archery set for my birthday—I think I was eight. I've never thought of it as a particularly significant toy.
> T: Tell me about it.

P: Well, It was just a bow that shot arrows with suction tips on the end so the arrow would stick to its target. There was a cardboard bull's eye target that came with it.

T: Does it strike you that there is something missing in your imagery?

P: No. Like what?

T: The arrows. A bow isn't very effective without them.

P: (Chuckling) They're probably in my left hand. (Suddenly frowns)

T: What's the matter?

P: Jeez. I just remembered something.

T: What is it?

P: My mother. She took those arrows away from me. I shot them at some lamps in the living room. She caught me and got real mad. I guess she threw them away. I never got them back.

T: What do you feel about that?

P: Right now kind of mad. But I remember feeling guilty as hell at the time. I could have broken those lamps.

T: O.K. Is the image still clear?

P: Yes. I've got it.

(If the image had diminished, we would have spent some time energizing it before moving on.)

T: Fine. Now, I want you to stretch your imagination and bring that little nine year old you, little Hank, right into this room. Imagine that he's actually here with us now. What do you do or say in regard to him?

P: (With an expression of distaste) You want me to do something with him?

T: Yes. And/or speak to him.

P: (Squirming a bit) This is silly.

T: Actually, it's crazy. Can you risk being crazy for a few minutes?

P: (Sighing) I suppose. What do you want me to say?

T: Anything you like.

P: I guess I'd say, 'Hi. Come on in.'

T: Say it directly to him.

P: Oh, jeez. Hi, Henny, come on in.

(I assumed that "Henny" was a nickname for young Hank and immediately began using it along with the patient. I was later informed that it was a term of endearment bestowed on him by his mother.)

> T: Any change in your image of Henny now that you've brought him closer?
>
> P: No. He's just standing there real stiff. He looks so scared. (There were several seconds of silence and, then, a flow of tears.) Poor little guy (said softly).
>
> T: Now, you're feeling.
>
> P: I can't believe I'm crying like this. I want to hug the little guy but I can only touch this one side of him. It's like he's only half a person.
>
> (More tears)
>
> T: Why don't you tell Henny that you'd like to hug him and be close to him. Ask him if he'll face you so you can.
>
> P: Hey, Henny...it's o.k. I just want to hug you. You can turn around for that.
>
> (Ten seconds of silence)
>
> T: What's happening?
>
> P: (Sadly) He says he's not allowed to show his other side.
>
> T: O.K. How about asking him if you and he can work together toward the goal of meeting each other face to face?
>
> P: (Softly) Will you let me work with you so we can be face to face? (Pause) He says 'yes." (A sigh of relief)
>
> T: Terrific. Why don't you make a date with Henny right now to meet at your next therapy session?

Meeting the Inner Child

As the foregoing illustrates, Inner Child imagery, like all secret missions, begins with a relaxation procedure. This readies the private eye or inner observer for his work. I am delineating the steps which follow relaxation in the form of instructions which I would give to a therapist treating a client. If you are not in therapy and are working with a trusted other, that person can assume the role of the therapist as outlined below.

If you are working entirely alone you will have to set up your tape recording so that substantial pauses are allowed for you to form your images and to interact with them. For the follow-up procedure you will need to review your imagery in the state of ordinary consciousness and dialogue with your private eye about it.

Here are the steps:

1. Reassure the client that any image produced or even failure to produce an image will provide useful therapeutic information . Unlike other tasks in the client's life, this is one in which he cannot fail. Also encourage the client to abstain from censoring the images.

2. Instruct the client to get in touch with an image of himself as a child. Stick to this simple direction. If the patient seeks more information from you say, "Any image of you as a child will do."

3. Allow the client plenty of time to develop the image. Imaging clients are extremely sensitive to therapist impatience. If it is obvious to you that the client is censoring, remain patient and ask about it in the follow-up.

4. When the client indicates contact with an image, ask for a detailed description. If details are not given, request them. By doing so, you are helping the client to clarify and intensify the image and, probably, deepening her trance level. Also get details about background.

5. Ask the client, while keeping the image in view, what feelings he is aware of.

6. Ask the client if the image connects with a specific experience from childhood.

7. Instruct the client to bring the imaged child into the treatment room. Suggest that he physically and/or verbally interact with the Child.

8. If unfinished business between the client and image remains, have them agree upon a time and place to meet for further work. Unless the client has had considerable experience with imagery, it is better to plan this for the next scheduled therapy session.

9. No imagery session is complete without a follow-up discussion aimed at helping the patient to clarify and integrate the experience.

The Follow-Up Procedure

The follow-up is most important and sessions should be planned to allow time for it after every imagery task. It enables the therapist to determine how the client interprets what has transpired and to correct for any negative or destructive aspects, be they real or projected. It is also the proper time for the therapist to make well thought out interpretations if necessary.

One of the beauties of this technique is that the images impact the imagist with strong messages which for the most part are readily self interpreted, diminishing the need for the therapist's input. If you are working without a therapist or helper, the follow-up will consist of a rational review of the imagery experience.

Follow-up procedure is generally open ended and begins with the eliciting of the client's thoughts and feelings about the experience. The therapist should take responsibility for keeping this evaluative discussion squarely within the framework of viewing the imagery as a production of which the client was entirely in charge.

Many clients tend to avoid responsibility for what was experienced by saying, "you made me see such and such" or "I just did what you told me to do." They must be reminded that, within the limitations of what was suggested, they chose the particular image and directed the action associated with it.

The symbolic significance of the image is also a matter to be considered in the follow-up. Details, like the bow in Hank's imagery can be fraught with meaning. Issues and meanings which remain unclear can be dealt with at the next session by having the patient recontact the images.

To further elucidate, here is the transcription of my follow-up with Hank.

(Hank opens his eyes, rubs them with his fingertips and runs his hands through his hair.)

> T: What are your thoughts and feelings about that experi-
>   ence?
> P: I can't believe I was actually crying. It's really weird.
> T: Why do you think it's weird? You seemed genuinely sad
>   for that little boy.
> P: I was, but...that's like feeling sorry for myself.
> T: That's right. Are you not allowed to?
> P: It's not like I was beaten or starved or anything.
> T: There are other kinds of pain.
> P: Yeah...I was such a little soldier...standing straight...not
>   even looking like a kid.
> T: You know, when I suggested that you image yourself as a
>   child, there was a wide range of images you could have
>   come up with. You could have visualized yourself at an
>   earlier or later age and in a multitude of different settings.
>   Why do you suppose you chose this particular image?
> P: I didn't really think of it as a choice. I guess two or three

pictures flashed before me and this one just seemed to take over.

T: Some part of you made the selection.

P: I guess my unconscious...I don't think I would have been able to handle an image of me in a real helpless state. At least, in this one I'm trying to stand tall. I guess that's why I have the little bow. (Pause) I'm trying to look strong and aggressive.

T: Is it aggression or defense?

P: (Angrily) It doesn't matter. I'm not going to be successful at either. I don't even have any goddam arrows!

T: Your mother took them. You're angry with her?

P: She wouldn't let me be a regular kid.

T: You said at one point the arrows might be in the hand on your hidden side.

P: Yeah. That must be the "real kid" side of me. I had to keep that part of me hidden.

T: Even from yourself.

P: Yeah...well...You know...I must be really afraid to be aggressive.

T: Do you have an idea about why that's so?

P: I don't know. Maybe because my father was aggressive and was such an ass hole.

T: You told me he didn't do so well at controlling your mother.

P: (Thoughtfully) That's right.

T: Do you suppose she took his arrows too?

P: She sure knew how to get to him. He didn't seem able to get back at her for the things she did but I'm sure he would have liked to.

T: And you?

P: Yeh...I suppose. I didn't let myself think about how much I resented her.

T: Do you suppose shooting arrows at her table lamps had something to do with resentment?

P: I...yeah...it fits. It seemed innocent at the time but I have to doubt it now. (Laughs) I guess I was trying to put her lights out. (Pause) I guess I think that other side of my kid is dangerous.

T: Well, it's a part of you that you need to get to know and accept. You've tried all these years to disown it but it hasn't gone away and it won't. The next time you meet with your Kid we can work on this.

When Hank finally confronted his Inner Child full face, he

was alarmed by the amount of hostility he found there but it was a major breakthrough toward the resolution of his problem. He was flooded with awareness of how "used' he felt at the hands of his mother. His resentment and mistrust of her carried over to other women on whom he found it necessary to depend.

His dependency on his wife became more problematical for him after she herself became a mother. As she operated out of that newly established role, Hank became more sensitive about the demands and expectations she placed on him. Some of her efforts to get him involved more fully in the parenting process were construed as replays of his mother's manipulations which deprived him of his childhood.

Hank's angry, aggressive feelings toward his wife escalated. His defense system operated to keep those feelings out of his awareness but could not contain the anxiety associated with them.

The truth of his psychological state was revealed in the bedroom where he could not maintain an erection long enough to ejaculate inside his wife's vagina. Once again, mother had deprived Hank of his arrows. He could function adequately only with someone who did not represent mother such as the younger woman with whom he was having an affair.

All of this was brought to light and worked through primarily via imagery. The Inner Child was both a source for uncovering repressed material and a vehicle for resolving emotional conflicts.

Hank discovered, as we all must, that liberation from one's childhood lies not in shucking off the Child within us as a snake sheds its skin but in fully embracing it with all of its pain, joys and sorrows just as an unconditionally loving parent would. No matter how well or poorly we fared with the parents who raised us, we ourselves have the power to give to that Child what every child most longs for—total acceptance.

From the Therapist's Notebook: Meeting the Kid

For many years I forgot the Time of Dreams. I would have told you there was no such time. It went out with the junk from the attic that we burned and gave away. Only a wisp of memory remained, fleetingly triggered by the lilting flight of a butterfly, the tickle of grass against the soles of bare feet, or the voice of a stranger echoing the loving voice that called me in for dinner.

These and many other little things called me back time and again, but I killed the Dreams in utero. I wouldn't allow them to emerge again. I had grown beyond all that. I was the Realist.

I had no difficulty remembering the Freud stuff. How

classic I was—a child obedient to all pronouncements made to him. I remembered the pain of it better than anything else. Sad Child, Hurt Child, gasping for air, cringeing in the face of my enemies— Scared Child, Sweet Child, wanting everyone to love everyone, knowing that they don't. I remembered all of that. How strange that I forgot the loveliness of the Time of Dreams.

"Close your eyes," the man said, "and allow an image—any image—to appear." It sounded so simple. Why did I find my mouth dry and my palms sweaty? What was there to fear in an image? It was all pretty silly anyway. I was sure others in the group felt the same way. Hocus pocus time—this guy thought he was going to do me some magic. Like hell! But why was I afraid?

"Take your time," the man said. "Don't censor. Accept whatever comes and stay with it. You can learn from it no matter what it is."

I waited, bemused. Nothing happened. I told myself nothing would. Ho-hum and a barrel of bullshit.

I already knew how to do therapy. I was good at it. So why was I exploring a method imported from California, home of the kooky therapeutic fringe? I wished I were somewhere else. My heart was pounding. Oh, God, suppose...

Then, he came. Against my will, he came - Sad Child, Scared Child, Hurt Child. One glimpse and I understood my apprehension. It was him I had been fearing.

He was the one, above all, I didn't want to encounter. He was the one I knew I would encounter. How had I managed to forget? Imagery was nothing new. I had seen this guy many times before. The Archangel of Depression.

He was my Feel Bad Image and here he was in all his glory, ready to make me look like a jerk in front of my colleagues. He would undo me. He would reveal me to be the fraud I was. No confident, wise, intact therapist. Just Sad Child, Scared Child, Hurt Child. I told him to go away.

"Let the image do what it wants," the man said. "Just stay with it. See if it changes. See if it takes you somewhere."

The pain was too much. I told the image again to go away. Then, I remembered the rules of our game. The more I would tell him to leave, the longer he would linger. He would dig in his heels until I was bathed in self pity. I didn't want that.

I decided to go with the new game. Leave him alone and see what happens. Some part of me screamed that this was not a wise decision.

With difficulty I focused all of my attention on the Child. I was astonished when he beckoned to me with a wave of his arm. Was I making this happen? It didn't feel that way but, of course,

I was. I chuckled at this trick of my mind but I followed his sign.

In some strange fashion we seemed to be traveling. I felt something like a rush of wind around me and had a sense of rapidly changing geographic patterns. The image was drawing me into another dimension and I lost notice of and concern for everything around me.

We burst upon a scene of sunshine, blue sky and green grass. Two children were at play. I recognized them instantly. One was my beloved Mary Jo and the other me—only this me was not Sad, Scared and Hurt. This me was happily, busily at play with intensity of purpose. This was the lost me of the Dream Time.

My playmate and I were transforming our reality with frequency and ease. We transported ourselves to the Wild West, to the open seas, to the jungles. We nurtured stuffed animals, all of whom had names and talked to us. We invented friends and villains, beasts and monsters according to our needs. We saw them clearly and, depending on their nature and our whims, fought them, saved them, killed them and loved them.

The wonder and beauty of the Time of Dreams came back to me full force at that moment. Sad Child, Scared Child, Hurt Child had a brother whom I had effectively forgotten, an unbounded Child of Joy.

I saw his box of toy soldiers, his favorite playthings. He breathed life into them and they became people, actors in the fantasies he constructed during long hours of lone play. They were not confined to the military roles suggested by their uniforms. They became cowboys, gangsters, policemen and firemen with the greatest of ease.

I was observing the secret of my survival. I knew immediately why I had not completely succumbed to Sad Child, Scared Child, Hurt Child. I knew that in those days of my innocence I had discovered the supreme survival mechanism - that I had ultimately transcended the pain and fear through my own imagination. What a precious gift for me to have lost—no, abandoned—the marvelous gift for imagining.

The messages came back to me. They had been there from early on. Obedient child that I was, I never questioned them.

"Growing up means leaving the Time of Dreams. All that imaginative play keeps you from being socially well adjusted. You spend too much time alone. You spend too much time in make-believe; that's not what life's all about. You've got to be tough; you've got to be hard to make it in life. That's sissy stuff. You're a boy!"

I remembered the day I packed the soldiers away in a tin box for the last time. Their depleted condition manifested the richness and intensity of my fantasy life.

Those little men reflected more wear and tear than actual veterans of combat. Paint was flaking, chips and dents were everywhere and some were even missing appendages. They had been the best and dearest of comrades and I wept in grief as I sealed their tomb of tin.

In secret I placed the box at the bottom of the garbage container, not wanting to share my decision or their fate with anyone. I was eleven years old. I cried myself to sleep. It was the end of the Time of Dreams.

"Now that you're back in your ordinary state of consciousness," said the man, "think about what you learned from your image."

It had been a revelation. Once I had known a world apart from the material universe and it had been a realm of comfort, healing and learning. I had turned my back on it in the name of growing up but, surely, it was still there. I wanted it in my life once more.

CHAPTER SIX

THE WORST SCENARIO

There is a fascinating sequence in the 1933 RKO film classic *King Kong* as movie producer Carl Denham played by Robert Armstrong and the crew of his ship "Venture" sail toward a mysterious island where Denham hopes to find and film a movie about a giant ape no white man has ever seen. He has brought along a needy, beautiful young woman who is to star in the motion picture and who is also to serve as "bait" to attract Kong.

Aboard ship, Denham has his ingenue do a screen test in which she is to imagine something so huge and frightening that it paralyzes her with fear. Actress Fay Wray, playing the girl, Ann Darrow, obviously succeeds in vividly imaging the terror that ultimately awaits her.

The scene exemplifies the technique of "worst scenario" imagery. Paradoxically, imaging that which most terrifies us can produce therapeutic gains. The technique is simple - the subject is asked to imagine something disturbing and to somehow deal with it.

For the average client, of course, this need not be anything as ostentatious as King Kong, though some would prefer facing the big fellow over their own inner fears. It is a type of imagery which requires thoughtful planning if it is to be therapeutic.

With a phobic patient, it isn't difficult to come up with a prescribed image but, more often than not, the imagist's "worst thing" is something vague or completely unknown. This factor renders this particular technique difficult to perform without the assistance of a therapist or someone who knows the imagist well.

The worst scenario to be dealt with may be a scene from the past or a projection into the future. It may be a loss or a traumatic event. Very often, it is connected with giving up a heavily relied upon defense. Sometimes the worst scenario is the patient getting what she thinks she most wants.

The Case of the Invisible Lady

Emily, a forty year old woman who came to me full of angry depression but unaware of it, provides an example of how the Worst Scenario Technique can be used. She was blaming her discontent on everyone and everything outside of herself.

According to Emily, her husband, mother and children had all been taking advantage of her caretaking nature for years without showing the slightest appreciation or concern for her needs. She was fed up and expressing a desire to get away from all of them. She made repeated references to running away, apparently unaware of how incongruent that idea was with her desperate desire for more attention.

Emily said the only thing which stopped her from taking off was a lack of money. Repeatedly she used the statement, "I'd like to just disappear."

She had tried to compensate for the lack of love and attention from her family by taking a lover but he turned out to be just like the rest of them. He had a wife and children of his own and gave them priority over Emily even when she was in greatest need of his company.

At the time of our initial session, this lady was angry with the whole world, including me. She stated that she didn't know why she was bothering with therapy because she wouldn't be able to depend on me either. She just about had herself convinced that she didn't need anybody and would be happiest taking care of no one but herself.

At our second session, I introduced her to imagery. Capitalizing on her phrase, "I'd like to just disappear," I guided her into a moderately relaxed state and told her I would like her to imagine vividly along with me as I began a story with her as the central person. I informed her that, at some point in the story, I would turn it over to her and she could finish it as she liked.

"We've just completed our session," I began, "and, on the way out, you stop at the rest room. As you go to wash your hands you notice lying on the sink a ring with a large, unusual stone. As you examine it you see there are minute carvings on the stone which look like hieroglyphics. It's a very magical looking ring.

"You feel compelled to try on the ring and slip it on your finger. As you do, you are totally astonished to see your reflection in the mirror disappear. You look down at your hands but don't see them. You look at your body and it is not there. Amazingly, the ring has made you invisible.

"Now, you take over."

As you see, in the context of the imagery, the patient has been given what she says she wants - invisibility. I have seen o.k. people have a lot of fun with this kind of fantasy, usually by creating a little mischief.

Invisibility would give many of us license to act out some of our forbidden impulses a fantasy of that can be delicious. Imaged invisibility usually invites themes that are voyeuristic, sexual, exploitative or grandiose. As you shall see, Emily was too emotionally impoverished to incorporate these themes into her imagery and develop them.

Here is her imagery verbatim:

Smiling. "This is great." Her voice level remains rather low.

"I go on out to my car and chuckle as I think about how confused your secretary is going to be because she doesn't see me leave...I sit in the car thinking about what I want to do...My husband's always refusing to take me out and I tell him I'm going to go sit in a bar but I never do...I can do that, now, though...There's a certain bar I've always wondered about because it looks so exotic from the outside...I decide to go there...

"I enter the bar through a bamboo curtain...The decor is oriental...I take a seat and look around...Not many people there...It's too early...Several couples seem to be having fun...I...I envy them. There are a couple of good looking men sitting at the bar. I think about whispering in one's ear but I see he's wearing a wedding ring...All of a sudden, I don't like the place.

"The beach is where I like to go...I drive there. Nobody seems to notice the driverless car going along the highway. They probably think it's advertising something if they notice at all.

Sighing. "I'm at the beach now. Families are picnicking. Everybody seems to have someone...I decide to go for a swim...I wade in near a handsome man...Of course, he doesn't know I'm there...I move toward him but he's heading back to shore. Oh, hell, I might as well take a swim...Now, I'm swimming out away from everyone...I feel utterly alone...

Voice drops. "I'm out pretty far...If I drowned, I'd never be found...The thought bothers me, somehow...It looks stormy...I decide to go in.

"Back at the car, I find a package lying beside it. I pick it up and open it after I get in. It's...It's money—a lot of it. Several thousand dollars. There's nothing to indicate who it might belong to and, certainly, no one can see me with it. I drive off.

"After I drive a few blocks, I take off the ring because I don't want to be stopped with the money in the car. All the way home, I'm thinking about what I want to do with the money.

Suddenly, I'm scared. I know I could use it to go somewhere but I don't know where to go. I'm all confused. I've got to have time to think.

"I arrive at home and hurry to the hall closet. I take down a shoe box and put the money and the ring inside. I'm just going to leave it there until I think about things."

Now, here's a lady who really doesn't know how to enjoy invisibility! She grew obviously more depressed as her imagery unfolded. At the end, her head hung low and her voice was barely above a whisper.

In our follow-up, Emily noted that she had felt an initial excitement when it was suggested that she had become invisible. She had a momentary sense of freedom but it quickly gave way to confusion and despair. She concluded, "No wonder I can't get out of my rut. I can't even imagine doing it!"

The imagery made conscious for this patient her need for greater visibility, not invisibility. It taught her an enlightening lesson—that her dependency needs were much stronger than she had believed. It wasn't the lack of funds or the attitudes of others which was keeping her stuck. It was her own indecisiveness, insecurity and passivity. Even when given extraordinary power, she was unwilling (unable from her perspective) to use it.

In this case, the imagery served to confront the patient with the depth of her depression and some of the defenses surrounding it. It enabled us to go to work on her poor self esteem and fear of being powerful.

In worst scenario imagery, the mission of the private eye is to encounter whatever the patient finds scary. The way this encounter is played out imaginally usually elucidates the patient's real life defensive measures, such as Emily's avoidance mechanisms. Sometimes, the imagery breaks through the defenses to such an extent that repressed material is recalled or new insights are gained, making it an excellent uncovering technique.

In addition to uncovering, this type of imagery evokes related feeling states, such as Emily's depression. It also directs attention to the kinds of symbols with which the patient needs to work for problem resolution. One of the symbols we followed up on was Emily's closet wherein she kept hidden her unacknowledged and unused resources.

The skilled therapist structuring this type of imagery will rely heavily on diagnostic data and therapeutic intuition. If diagnosis is uncertain, the technique can be helpful in clarifying it.

This can often be accomplished by suggesting to the client imagery that is vague but carries the potential for revelation. For example, he can be the recipient of some form of communication. Who is it from? What does it say? What kind of feeling/thinking response does it evoke? What action is taken?

Variations on this theme include getting a package or gift; receiving an award; opening up an old trunk stored in the attic; entering a cave; diving deep into the sea; or exploring a basement. All of these scenarios invite contact with that which is unknown, hidden or secret.

The Case of the Finger Crossing Maiden

One of my clients, 18 year old Kendra, was bright, pretty and composed as she described having some mild episodes of anxiety since going off to college. She attributed the symptoms to the fact that her parents were getting divorced, following her father's involvement with another woman. She was concerned about her mother's adjustment to the situation because, although mother kept a stiff upper lip, Kendra knew she was feeling insecure and frightened.

Kendra was so controlled that it was difficult to assess the seriousness of her problem. She was obviously the kind of person she described her mother to be—an internalizer of feelings. She acknowledged that the two of them were extremely close.

Following relaxation, I suggested that Kendra go to her imaginary mailbox and find a letter. She did so, recognizing immediately that it was from her mother. It read as follows:

"You are not to worry about me, Kendra. I can handle this disgusting situation just fine. Your father has simply lived up to his male nature and turned, as they all do around middle age, to someone much younger. He'll live to regret it but I won't care. I would never let him touch me again.

"I still have you, my friends and my rose garden and can be very happy if I get a reasonable settlement. I just want you to take care of yourself. I never want you to go through this kind of unhappiness.

"Keep your fingers very tightly crossed."

In follow-up Kendra perceived the letter as expressing the kind of selfless concern typical of her mother. Noticing that the girl had her arms entwined across her chest and her legs tightly crossed, I asked her what the last sentence meant to her.

She replied, as expected, that crossed fingers are for good luck. Then, I asked what kind of magic she was promoting with her crossed arms and legs. She became flustered but went on to say that her mother had always been very protective and had encouraged her to be on guard, partiuclarly around males. She said she kept her legs crossed to ward off sexual feelings.

"Mine or yours?" I asked and we were off and running in the area of Kendra's intense sexual anxiety and the compulsive defenses by which she "protected" herself. She said later she had not planned to talk about her sexual fears and it is doubtful we would have were it it not for the imagery. It provided an inroad into the girl's central problem which was being exacerbated by the parents' divorce.

The Case of the Displaced Fear

When the diagnosis is clear, the imagery can easily be structured around more specific symbols. The anxious patient can be placed in the kind of situation which arouses his anxiety. Persons or objects which trigger discomfort can be confronted.

To illustrate, Corey, a young college student consulted me about his extreme anxiety over interpersonal involvement with females. He perceived himself to be shy and passive. He had never been able to make a date with a girl and could only tolerate female companionship in group situations. Consciously, he construed this to reflect a pathological fear of rejection.

I asked him to image taking a drive in the country and having his car break down on an unfamiliar country road. Soon, another car approaches and stops. A lone, young female emerges.

Corey took over the fantasy and found, to his surprise, that the young woman was friendly toward him and offered him a ride to where he could call for help. His anxiety was at a peak as he got into the car beside her. Then, shockingly, all hell broke loose.

The patient was seized by lust for the girl and grabbed her, locking her into a passionate embrace. She resisted and he began forcing himself on her. At that point, Corey brought himself out his trance, saying he had harbored no intention of having the imagery work out that way.

The imagery tapped into the real source of his anxiety around women. He did not fear rejection from females so much as his own repressed sexual/aggressive impulses toward them. This outwardly passive young man was a wolf in sheep's clothing. We were able to go to work on that.

By repeating such imaged experiences, new and different behaviors and attitudes on the part of the patient can be developed. A frightening image such as this one can be worked through time and again with different outcomes.

The Case of the Absolute Hero

In imagery, the client can be deprived of some power which is overused or abused. If money is the tool for manipulation, she can be made destitute. If it is sexual attractiveness, that can be rendered irrelevant.

Conversely, the client can be given some power which is lacking. The victim can become persecutor, the dependent person can be made independent and the fat person, thin. In each case, the therapeutic lessons lie in what is done or not done, felt or not felt under the altered circumstances.

With Trevor, for example, I designed a scenario inimical to his narcisistic personality structure. He was a twenty-eight year old musician, playing with a rock group.

This man was extraordinarily handsome and spent a large part of each day on body building activities. He boasted frequently of his "star power" and interpreted every booking of the band as a step toward "the big time."

He gave no credit to his fellow musicians, nor to his worshipful wife, Claudia, who catered to him during the day and diligently sat stageside every night watching him perform. Trevor displayed little capacity for recognizing, much less relating to the feelings of his wife or others.

His imagery was structured around a walk in the woods with Claudia. They became lost and were descended upon by a gang of pirates. A strugggle ensued during which Claudia was knocked unconscious and left for dead. Trevor's leg was hurt so that he could not run away and he was dragged off as a prisoner.

Trevor was invited to take over at that point and completed the fantasy by making himself a veritable Superman who vanquished his captors and escaped with their booty. He completely forgot his leg and his injured wife as he drove the pirates' truck, loaded with treasure, back toward civilization.

After some follow-up discussion, he agreed to repeat the imagery, this time allowing Claudia to regain consciousness and rescue him. He started in that direction but, before long, was back to being the super hero. He could not grant Claudia that much importance, even in fantasy. These images became the spring-board for our early therapeutic work on his narcissism.

The Case of the Unscalable Wall

If you are working with imagery outside of therapy you can decide on an appropriate person, problem or setting for you to explore during your exercise. If you are a therapist you can give your clients any kind of problem solving task to image. It can relate to their problem directly as when it is suggested they encounter a specific person with whom they are in conflict or it can relate to their problem symbolically.

To one particularly self defeating client, I gave the task of finding a way over or through a wall on the other side of which was something she very much wanted. (I did not specify what it was.)

She engaged in long, involved imagery in which she tried one thing after another to surmount that wall. Nothing worked, so we stopped after about fifteen minutes.

In follow-up, the client stated the imagery had been a revelation to her. She could see that she would do anything to prevent getting what she wanted. She was afraid to even know what she wanted. This is why she could not allow herself to get over the wall.

An occasional client tells me that he made a deliberate attempt to create imagery that had no relation to his problems. It doesn't work.

Every image is a projection of some aspect of ourselves and, as it unfolds, reveals us for who and what we are. Persons seeking to elude such revelation in their imagery are amazed to discover that it can't be done as long as they choose to be accepting of and honest in reporting about the images that appear to them. The private eye, like Sherlock, observes what is there and what is there always provides clues to what is really going on.

From the Therapist's Notebook: A Bad Scene

'I'm willing to face it," I said to myself. "I'm willing to face whatever, for me, is the scariest thing. I'm ready to learn from it."

With that, I closed my eyes and sent Sherlock on a mission to bring back my worst fear in the form of an image. It was a positive period of my life. I felt strong—invincible.

It seemed a long time before anything began to stir. The first thing I noticed was a sound like the distant roar of a crowd. It's quite unusual for me to have auditory images apart from visualization.

The scene developed slowly. It was a large audotorium. A

blue and pink haze floated to the vaulted ceiling. The crowd was not cheering—they moaned sorrowfully.

I was aware of an extremely bright light shining directly down on me. The place was cold and I shivered. I became aware of being dressed in shorts.

My vision cleared and I knew I was in a boxing arena. The ropes were ruby red. The damp canvas was stained with ruddy smears. My opponent was a huge, faceless creature.

"This is not so bad," I told myself. "I used to box a little in high school. I never got hurt. I can handle this. Surely it's not my scariest thing."

I wondered why the crowd was so somber. I wondered why I was so cold.

The clang of the bell was sharp and clear. I came out of my corner.

It was then I discovered that I could not lift my arms. I could not defend myself. My opponent began hammering at me. It dawned on me that the image was not about boxing. It was about helplessness.

Sherlock had gone to the heart of the matter. I dread the thought of being unable to protect myself, do for myself, take charge of my life. I felt a heaviness in the pit of my stomach.

Well, I had asked for it. I vowed to stay with the image and try to learn from it. What could it possibly teach me? It seemed structured to inform me of what I already know. When you're helpless, you're chopped liver.

The beating started out bruising, moved to lacerating and became bone crunching. I could feel my insides being torn from their moorings. Blood trickled, then poured from my facial orifices. I endured until I knew the next blow would kill me.

It was then that I turned to the crowd that seemed to be suffering with me. "Help!" I called. "Won't somebody please help me?"

To my surprise people began to move forward. Men came into the arena and escorted my opponent away. Several women came and cradled me. My head rested against the bosom of a matronly Jewish lady.

Suddenly the image was gone. I returned to ordinary consciousness feeling as if I had really been battered.

Having reviewed it many times, I now get the lesson. Being helpless and dependent has fearful elements for many of us. My terror of it goes far beyond that normal kind of response.

The reason is in the imagery, though it took me a while to figure it out. What makes dependency intolerable to me is my unwillingness to ask for help. I had to know the death blow was coming before I asked for assistance from that sympathetic audience. Once I asked, help was abundant and effective.

I could maintain my well being and avoid situations of dire dependency if would learn to give into it sooner. I need to see the doctor when I start to cough rather than wait until I have pneumonia.

Imagery is symbolization in action. The persons, places and things which the client encounters have meaning beyond what they seem to represent literally.

Imagery taps into the unconscious much the same as dreams. Every form that appears deserves a second look to determine what it represents beyond the obvious.

CHAPTER SEVEN

CODED
MESSAGES

During my high school and college years, I worked as a messenger for Western Union. The telegram was a dying form of communication at that time but the unexpected arrival of one at a residence still had the power to arouse anxiety in the recipient. It was generally regarded as an "urgent" message, likely to contain bad news. On numerous occasions, as the bearer of such tidings, I was made to feel less than welcome at the doorstep.

Messengers bearing disagreeable news have never been popular figures. In the days of despotic rulers, it was a high risk job. If the message was upsetting enough, there was a good chance that the messenger would be slain on the spot just for bringing it.

In Greek and Roman mythology, one messenger rose to the rank of a minor deity. The Greeks called him Hermes and the Romans called him Mercury. He was the messenger of the gods.

Mercury is pictured as a youth wearing a winged hat, winged sandals and carrying the caduceus, a wand with two serpents twined around it. He is particularly interesting because of his multi-faceted makeup.

In addition to delivering the edicts of the higher powers, Mercury, noted for his inventiveness, was the god of science and commerce. He was also clever, deceptive, and wiley, attributes which qualified him to be the patron of travelers, rogues, vagabonds and thieves.

Like Mercury, symptoms, no matter what form they take, are messengers. Also like Mercury, they can be roguish and deceitful. They present a challenge to our private eyes and are usually unwelcome inasmuch as they are sent to inform us that something is amiss in our lives.

Their encoded message is highly informative if we can bring ourselves to decipher it. It tells us about our state of being while also describing the healing defenses and preventive strategies that our mind/body system is using to fight off disease.

Our cultural mind-set and the predominant medical philosophy is to get rid of symptoms as quickly as possible. Pain and discomfort are looked upon as intolerable afflictions rather than as important messages from higher powers. A quick eradication of them via chemical intervention is the preferred solution but, if that doesn't work, there is always the surgeon's knife.

Symptom related imagery encourages us to decipher the message embedded in our symptoms. We can learn from them a good deal more than just which of our organs happens to be out of whack.

Often, they are telling us that our whole lifestyle is out of whack or that we need to make changes in certain attitudes or behaviors. If we become hastily involved in minimizing or avoiding them at any cost, we shall not hear the secret wisdom they transmit.

How To Do Symptom Imagery

The imagery technique described in this chapter, prescribes a meeting between our private eye and the crafty Mercury, appearing in the form of whatever mental or physical symptoms we carry around. The mission is to decode his message and to put the information to use in whatever way is best for us.

This does not mean denying ourselves relief from pain and discomfort but it does mean actively encountering and working with these phenomena rather than passively waiting for someone to wave a magic wand that will vanquish them. Many chronic pain sufferers end up doing just that.

This type of imagery focuses our attention on our symptoms and translates them into a form which we can manipulate in various ways. We do this from the viewpoint that our symptoms are an expression of some part of ourselves which can help us by pointing out imbalance in our lives. We who have ears to hear what they are saying can profit from listening attentively.

The general procedure for symptom related imagery can be presented by the therapist in the following manner. Those working outside of a therapeutic relationship can modify the instructions for self use if no partner is available.

1. After relaxation, have the client focus mentally on the symptom to be worked with (headache, depression,

erectile dysfunction, physical pain, insomnia, obesity, anxiety, etc.).

2. Tell the client to allow an image representing the symptom to appear. Remind her that it can be anything at all and should be accepted uncritically whether it seems related to the symptom or not.

3. When the client is in touch with an image, ask her to describe it out loud in detail. (Remember, the more detail you elicit, the more vivid the image is likely to be.)

4. Inquire regarding what the client feels like doing with or about what is being imaged. Encourage her to act on those feelings imaginally and to report on what that experience is like.

5. Suggest that the client schedule a specific time and place for a subsequent meeting with the image, thank it for appearing and say good-bye.

6. Discuss in follow-up.

After all imagery exercises but especially after symptom imagery, I encourage clients to draw their images. Drawing has a way of giving the images greater validity. The mental energy of imaging is converted into something material, something more concrete. Sometimes, while drawing, clients recall something about the image which they neglected to describe.

Most clients draw immediately after the exercise. I keep pads of paper, pencils and crayons on my desk for this purpose. Some prefer to make their drawings at home and I am o.k. with that choice.

There are some clients who refuse to draw at all. I understand their resistance very well. Thanks to some unpleasant experiences in art class in elementary school, I was left with a strong aversion to all forms of artistic expression. Until just a few years ago I thought of myself as someone who "can't draw."

While working with imagery, I began to take the risk of graphically representing my inner experiences. With no claim of artistic excellence, I can report, to my own surprise, that my pictorials are fairly reliable approximations of my imagery. I have joined the ranks of some of my clients who report that drawing an image is a different kind of experience than attempting to draw an external object.

With or without drawings, this type of imagery makes possible some exciting psychotherapeutic situations. The client, who has probably been endlessly reciting a litany of symptomatic conditions, now has a dynamic symbol to work with instead. His thoughts and feelings about that symbol and the ways he manipulates it become the therapeutic focus and moments of high drama can ensue.

The Case of the Ominous Goose

Todd, a nineteen year old college student, had begun having anxiety attacks shortly after taking up dormitory residence at one our area's universities. He was slight of build and highly intellectual. He excelled at academics.

He got along well with his peers, though he avoided close involvement with anyone. He was not athletically inclined and took some teasing about that from his jock roommate but they understood each other and accepted their differences.

Todd's episodes of panic frequently occurred at bedtime and occasionally in relatively unstructured social situations where people were just sitting around talking. He had no insight into their origin.

At our second session, I taught him relaxation. While he was in a light trance state, I suggested that he concentrate for a moment on his feelings of panic and allow an image representing those feelings to appear in his mind's eye. I cautioned him to accept whatever came, whether it seemed relevant or not.

In a few seconds, he reported visualizing a goose and said, "This is stupid."

"Good," I said, "all of your intelligence hasn't solved your problem, maybe some stupidity will. Please describe your goose."

Todd described a large, snow white goose. Somehow, he knew it to be a gander. It was hissing and appeared hostile. As the young man focused on it, he experienced a growing sensation of fear.

I asked what he would like to do with or about the goose and received the response, "Run from it!"

"Very well," I said. "Why don't you run and see what happens?"

There was a tightness in Todd's voice as he described his flight from the pursuing fowl. His body became tense and he gripped the arms of the chair.

"I'm running like hell," he said hoarsely, "but the damn thing's after me. It's honking and hissing. I has its wings spread out and its neck thrust forward. It looks wild and crazy. It wants to bite me. For some reason, I'm really scared of it."

I let Todd continue his flight for a time before I suggested that he stop running and face the goose, just to see what would happen. He acted on my suggestion and found that when he stopped, the gander stopped. Tuning in on his feeling state, he discovered that he was less afraid when facing the animal than when it was at his back.

The client was beginning to sense a slight feeling of control over his image but said he was too frightened to draw closer to it. Respecting his fear, I suggested he call out to the goose and ask why it had come to him.

Now deeply immersed in the imagery, Todd called out in a loud voice, "What are you doing here?"

A response came immediately and Todd repeated it. "I'm only good for plucking and eating."

"Ask what that has to do with your anxiety," I encouraged.

The reply was, "It's the only way to get me off your back."

With some urging on my part, Todd reluctantly thanked the attack goose for appearing and set a date to meet him again at our next therapy session.

At the beginning of our follow-up period, the client expressed surprise at how real his encounter with the goose had seemed. This is a common reaction of patients new to imagery, especially those who have strong intellectual defenses.

I asked Todd if he would draw his image while we talked. He set to work as I inquired about what the experience meant to him.

"It was pretty powerful," he said, pencil in hand. "I don't really understand the symbolism of the goose. It seems trite. I did have an encounter with a goose when I was maybe five or six but it wasn't all that traumatic."

"Tell me about it," I urged.

"My parents took my sister and me to visit some of their friends in Alabama. They had a country home with a pond. There were lots of animals on the grounds, including ducks and geese.

"I was running around, having a great time, when I guess I infringed on an old gander's territory. Like geese do, he came at me and scared me enough that I cried but my dad stepped between us so he never bit me. It doesn't seem particularly upsetting as I think about it now."

"What is your response to the goose saying it came to be plucked and eaten?" I asked.

Todd was absorbed in coloring his picture. "I guess that is about all geese are good for. I don't think I've ever eaten one. I haven't been a big eater since I got in my teens. I'd have to say I'm pretty finicky.

"The plucking part says to me that I've got to strip this symbol down and see what's behind it. Maybe eating means I've got to digest it, somehow—incorporate it."

Todd held up the finished drawing. He had managed to capture the hostile nature of his subject.

"Would you like to give him a name?" I asked.

"Oh, let's call him....let's just call him plain, old Bill."

Any symptom, be it primarily mental or primarily physical, can be imaged in this way. Sometimes the image is quite literal, as when an erectilely dysfunctional male visualizes his flaccid penis. Usually, as with Todd, the image is more symbolic.

In this instance, I chose to have the client symbolize his problem in its broadest definition, i.e., anxiety. I could have just as well had him symbolize some specific aspect of his anxiety such as his food phobia or his rapid, pounding heartbeat. Presumably, any of these avenues would lead to more or less the same destination.

Pain, regardless of its origin, is an excellent symptom for the imagery approach. One patient visualized his sinusitis as a cave subject to rockfalls which occluded the opening. A woman experienced her facial tic as a television set which distorted its broadcast images due to electrical surges. Another patient encountered his ulcer pain as a pirranha gnawing at its fishbowl, his stomach. Intuitively, patients come up with excellent symbols for their particular pain.

Likewise, coughs, diarrhea, constipation, fever and any other symptomatic condition can be symbolized. Calling up a picture of a specific, malfunctioning internal organ also provides a meaningful symbol of symptomatology.

A note of caution is worth repeating here. While it is appropriate to use imagery in conjunction with medical treatment of symptoms it should not be use in lieu of such treatment if the problem persists or is suggestive of serious illness.

Even if imagery alone is capable of curing an exceptional individual, none of us has any way of knowing if we are that exceptional person. There is no need to take this kind of risk because imagery works compatibly alongside of other established therapies.

The private eye's mission to confront Mercury is not complete until the messenger's communication is fully understood and responded to. Let's go on to explore the hidden message borne by Todd's goose.

The Decoding Process

Decoding is accomplished by approaching symptoms as messages from our nervous system. Most of us are cognizant of their warning function. We know they are telling us that something is wrong but there is even more to be learned from them..

In *Peace, Love and Healing* Bernie Siegel (1989) states:

> I think all of us need to discover our own myth. Often our diseases can help us to do that, for each person's experience of illness has a unique meaning, expressing something of the individuality of the person who is having the experience.

Symbolizing symptomatic messages is one way to decode them. It is through manipulation of the symbol that we come to know what the symptom is telling us, not only in terms of what's wrong but also in terms of what opportunities it presents for bio-psycho-socio-spiritual healing and enrichment.

After the client meets her symptom symbol, a therapeutic strategy can be worked out for cracking the code. A common form of coding is substitution, letting one thing stand for another.

The Case of the Cranial Dagger

Kevin's symptom was severe headaches for which no physical basis could be found. He had tried conventional and unconventional treatments with varying degrees of success. He had read about image therapy and was willing to "try one more thing." He was pretty burned out on all forms of treatment by that time but he worked extraordinarily well with imagery and had a successful course of therapy.

Kevin's image of his symptom was a dagger protruding from the top of his head. The weapon impressed him as being quite old. It had cryptic markings carved on the hilt.

When asked what he wanted to do with or about it, he said he wanted to sit very still and not disturb it. He asked it why it was there and it answered, confusingly, "To help you concentrate."

Certainly, the dagger was an appropriate and graphic symbol for the patient's "stabbing pain" but its mere descriptive relevance to what was being felt was not enlightening. Kevin's reluctance to manipulate the knife in any way and its stated purpose to help him concentrate suggested there were deeper meanings to be derived, once the code was broken. Its connection with an ancient form of writing like that found on the handle suggested that it might have some relevance to his past history.

The underlying message emerged as Kevin used his imagination to manipulate the symbol in ways which disturbed him. When he finally worked up the courage to place his hand on the knife handle, I suggested he was in a position to pull it out if he so desired. He broke into a sweat and trembled, repeating, "no, no, no."

"What's the matter?" I asked.

"I can't do it," he said, sobbing. "If I pull it out, all the stuff will come out. It's the only thing that keeps it in."

The way was opened for Kevin to eventually understand that his terrible headaches were a substitute for even more terrible memories and feelings he didn't want to deal with.

The dagger had told the truth. By keeping him concentrated on his pain, it distracted him from frightening emotional issues. It acted like a plug, keeping all of the scary stuff inside his head. As bad as the pain was, he unconsciously preferred to hold on to it rather than to have his repressed feelings and memories gush forth.

The patient ended up withdrawing the blade a fraction of an inch at a time, so as not to be swamped with feelings. His pain decreased and his depression increased. After a time, the headaches were no longer a factor. He was dealing with with his *real* pain —emotional pain.

The Secret of Code Cracking

The secret of code cracking is to get the client involved with his symptom symbol in a variety of ways. Some of the possibilities are:

1. Touch it.
2. Make it larger or smaller
3. Sit, climb or stomp on it.
4. Wear it.
5. Take it on an imaginary journey with you.
6. Share it with someone.
7. Eat it or feed it.
8. Change its color(s).
9. Wrestle with it.
10. Give it orders.
11. Obey or disobey it.
12. Love it.

Through these and other manipulations, the secret messages are wrung out of the symptom symbols. In addition, as the client finds it possible in imagery to exercise control over the symbol, a message is delivered back to her consciousness that the symptom itself can be managed.

The sense of helplessness to do anything about the illness is diminished. No longer acting the part of a helpless victim of disease, the client becomes less focused on finding the right magician to vanquish it. She gains awareness that she is an active participant in healing, an active partner of the physician or therapist.

A word of warning is in order regarding the client who may seek to destroy, throw away or otherwise dispose of the symbol before working with it. It is important that the therapist not allow this to happen until and if he is satisfied that a sufficient amount of working through with the symbol has taken place and that such action is justified.

Very rarely can the destruction of a symptom symbol be justified, because the wish to do so manifests a defense mechanism (denial) and is an attempt to avoid the necessary work. The client who is involved in taking control of a symptom does not find the total destruction of it important or necessry.

As you see, doing away with the symptom is not the immediate goal. Taking responsibility for it is the goal. The client achieves this by grappling with the symbol, not by demolishing it.

Plucking the Ominous Goose

Other, more complex forms of symbol manipulation are sometimes needed. This was the case with Todd whom you met earlier. Unraveling the message of the attack goose was, for him, a difficult, but worthwhile endeavor.

When he returned to my office for his second encounter with Bill, his anxiety level was high. He reported increased anxiety throughout the week. He had been trying, without much success, to decode Bill's hidden message.

At our session, Todd did not find it easy to relax. As soon as he bade Bill to come forward, the goose was there, looking larger and more menacing than before. He made the observation that, as long as he faced the animal, it would not attack. They remained at a stand-off, about ten feet apart.

The client became convinced that Bill intended to attack his genitals. I suggested that he ask Bill about this, but the bird would not answer. Todd was stuck in a truly uncomfortable place with his image.

I helped the young man break the deadlock by informing him that he did not have to depend on Bill's cooperation for answers. I reminded him that Bill was an artifact of his imagination and his very own creation in that sense. I told him that he had the power to merge right into the symbol and to view the world through Bill's eyes.

I utilized a count-down to ease Todd into a deeper state of trance, telling him that, at the count of ten, he would find that he had become Bill and would know all of Bill's inner experience. With each number I called out, I suggested that he was going deeper and deeper into a trance and merging more and more completely with Bill.

At the end of the counting, I said, "Now, tell me what it is like to be Bill."

Todd cranked his neck around a few times and hunched his shoulders. When he spoke, his voice was different, deeper.

"I feel frustrated. I can't get Todd to pay attention to me."

"He finds you threatening," I countered.

"That's why he needs to pay attention." Obviously, Todd was now completely absorbed into the aspect of himself represented by Bill. "I am a threat to him."

"What do you want exactly?" I asked.

"I want him to know that, if he doesn't take charge of me, he's going to get goosed. I'm going to shove my beak right up his rectum. If he tries to run away from me, that's exactly what is going to happen."

"And what if he doesn't run?" I inquired.

"Then," said Bill, "he can eat me. "I don't know why he's afraid to do that. When he eats me, I can be absorbed and I won't have to chase him around any more."

"That's what you want to happen?"

"Yes. Eating me won't hurt him. It will make him stronger. It will help him. He has me mixed up with someone else who did want to hurt him.

"Do you know who that is?" I asked hopefully.

"I don't know," said Bill. "Someone who acted like me. I don't know."

"Very well. Look at Todd and tell me what you see."

Following my suggestion, Todd was now looking at himself through the eyes of another aspect of his personality.

"He's really, really scared. He thinks something terrible is going to happen to him. He thinks it's going to happen in secret, under the covers so to speak, but it's still going to be terrible."

"And can you help him with his fear?"

"I can, if he'll stop running and pay attention. Otherwise, I'm just going to scare him more. I'm really trying to help him. If I don't pursue him, he'll never get to the bottom of things."

I instructed Todd to withdraw from Bill and resume his usual identity. Once back into himself, he was able to face Bill with much less anxiety. On my suggestion, he thanked him for his help and agreed to further meetings with him.

Some very important work was accomplished in this session. The technique of having the client "become" his image is a potent one. It is especially helpful when the client has difficulty manipulating the image.

Todd learned that his symptom, as symbolized by Bill, was basically trying to assist him despite its paradoxical and troubling nature. This is a valuable truth about symptoms, worthy of knowing.

They are saying, "Look, I'm doing unpleasant things to get your attention but that's because I have some terribly important things to teach you." Symptoms simultaneously communicate the disease and the cure.

The imaging process, without any accompanying rational explanation, taught the client that, like Bill, his anxiety was completely a production of his own nervous system and that, as such, it was at some level under his control. Once he stopped investing all of his energy in avoiding it and embraced it as his own creation, he began to understand and direct it.

In the end, it turned out that Bill was only superficially an encodement of the goose that frightened Todd when he was five. Through several subsequent encounters with Bill, a repressive barrier was broken down and the patient understood the true significance of his symbol.

It was revealed that Todd had never been very secure about his masculinity. Prior to his teens he was pudgy and not well coordinated physically. His intellectual interests and pursuits were beyond those of most of his peers. He was an agreeable child and tried to get along with everyone, but preferred the company of girls. This led to merciless teasing from some of the boys who called him "pussy" and "sissy." He was regarded as "weird" by members of both sexes.

At puberty, the boy experienced the usual surge of sexual energy and became an avid masturbator, entertaining mostly heterosexual fantasies. During this phase of his psychosexual development, he was sent to an all male Episcopal boarding school of high academic ranking. This seemed warranted on the basis of his advanced intellect.

Todd was stimulated and challenged by his new academic environment. He became totally enchanted with one of the teachers who also spent a lot of social time with him and several other boys.

In these informal sessions, it was not unusual for the teacher to partcipate in some grab-ass type play with the students.

After a time, Todd found the teacher's hand sometimes resting on his thigh under the table as they sat around it talking. He loved and respected the man too much to complain.

In retrospect, Todd realized that the teacher was having sex relations with several of the boys. He would not allow himself to think this while at the school but, during his second year there, the sexual intent became impossible to deny.

By that time, the teacher was making suggestive but non-commital comments like simply murmuring "Mmmmmm... mmmmm" while looking at Todd. The more acceptable pat on the ass became a goose. The patient began avoiding the social gatherings because of the anxiety they stirred up.

He was frequently tormented by fantasies in which the teacher attacked him sexually. The fantasies produced a mixture of fear and arousal.

The problem came to a head when the instructor cornered Todd in the bathroom and said, "When are you going to eat me, Todd? I know you want to eat me." The boy ran out in a panic, developed a severe case of flu and was sent home for several days. While at home, he begged his sympathetic parents to transfer him to a public school on the grounds that he was totally unhappy at the private school.

Being familiar with and sympathetic toward the boy's social adjustment problems, his mother and father allowed him to return to public school. He told them nothing of the sexual harrassment and, in fact, put it totally out of his mind until therapy was initiated and his imaged goose finally brought it all back.

During the time the incident remained suppressed, its residuals continued to present problems to Todd. He became obsessed with the notion that there was something decidedly feminine about him. His eating habits changed markedly and, to his delight, his pudgy little curves gave way to a string bean physique which he deemed to be more masculine even if not especially attractive.

In terms of peer relations, Todd remained pretty much a loner back in public school. He assiduously avoided his own sexuality and that of others. Masturbation became infrequent and he had little awareness of sexual fantasies or desires. He had platonic dating relationships with a couple of brainy girls during the remainder of high school.

Everything was held well in check until he started to college. Leaving his protected home environment and having to live closely with an "all man" type roommate began to break down the patient's brittle defenses. His self consciousness about his masculinity returned along with heaping doses of anxiety.

At casual gatherings, he unconsciously feared that something might happen "under the table." His bed time anxiety signalled his guardedness against the possible recurrence of homosexual fantasies.

The goose that pursued Todd was his sexual ambivalence. He both wanted and feared the intimacy symoblized by being goosed. At least, as long as he fled, he could view himself as being the innocent victim of a predator. To turn and willingly eat the goose cast him in the role of actively wanting to be intimate with his pursuer, a symbolic acknowledgment that the teacher had been right about him.

In time, Todd came to realize that he could incorporate his homosexual feelings and integrate them into his total personality structure without engaging in overt homosexual behavior and without having the rest of the world view him as a homosexual, which he was not. During one of his last imagery sessions, he ate the happily cooked goose.

Before making any of these connections, Todd had named the goose Bill. His teacher's name, it turns out, was Mr. William J. Fischer—Bill Fischer.

From the Therapist's Notebook: The Jitter Bird

In twenty-four hours I was to present my first major workshop. Just as I completed my preparation I began to obsess about the inadequacies of the entire concept. I was sure to be humiliated before my professional peers.

The tension and anxiety mounted over the next couple of hours. It suddenly dawned on me that I, an imagist, should certainly be able to do something ameliorative with that symptom.

I had to spend more time than usual to attain a good level of relaxation. Once there, I invited an image representing my immediate anxiety to appear. I got instant results.

An exceedingly tiny yellow bird began to flit all about in my field of vision. It was making high pitched sounds which, as my hearing sharpened, turned out to be frantic little phrases like "Oh, my gosh! Oh, dear! Me oh my! No, no, no!" They were uttered in staccato fashion.

"What's your name?" I asked, having trouble keeping it in view because of its fast movements.

"Jitters," it piped. "Jitters my name. Oh, yes! Me oh my."

"Jitters," I said, "I have something very important to do and you're making me nervous. I'm going to put you in a cage so you can't follow me to my workshop."

The bird's movements became even more accelerated. "Oh, no! Can't be done. Me oh my!"

"I don't need you," I said impatiently.

"Oh, sure. Sure you do," said Jitters. "If you didn't need me I wouldn't be here."

"Do you know why I need you?" I inquired.

"Oh, sure. You bet. I surely do."

"I want to learn from you. Tell me why I need you."

Jitters lit on the back of a chair and looked at me. His black b-b size eyes were crossed and the feathers about his head were disheveled. His speech, thank God was slowed.

"Don't you remember the warnings about conceitedness? With me along, you don't get too big for your britches."

The pipsqueak had hit the nail right on the head. My inner tapes were full of instructions on how to remain humble. My script calls for me to enjoy a measure of success but not too much. What better way to limit my performance than to become tense and anxious?

"You're absolutely right," I said, "but I'm ready for a change. I want to let you go."

"Oh, no. Can't do that all at once. You know better."

The wisdom of my images never ceases to amaze me. Jitters knew that deprogramming is a process. It was not realistic of me to think that I could totally divest myself of his services.

"I've got an idea," said the bird.

"What's that?"

"I'll leave a little reminder of me with you to keep you from getting a big head. Then, you can open the window and I'll fly out."

At that moment I had no idea what my image would do next but I trusted it.

"It's a deal," I said.

With that, Jitters flew up and perched on the top of my ear. I strained my eyes trying to watch him out their corners. It turned out that it wasn't necessary to see *what* he was doing.

I felt wetness behind my left ear and realized he had, as he suggested, left me with a reminder. He rode my ear as I went to the window and opened it. With a hearty "me oh my" he flew away.

I presented my workshop feeling calm and poised. Several times during the day when things were going especially well I felt something wet behind my ear. I couldn't help but chuckle when I did. The participants thought I was just in exceptionally good humor.

CHAPTER EIGHT

LOOKING-GLASS HOUSE

Following her fabulous adventures in Wonderland, Lewis Carroll's plucky heroine, Alice, becomes curious about the house which exists behind the mirror above her mantle. She calls it Looking-glass House.

It resembles her own house, but everything is in reverse and, she suspects, nothing is quite the same. To satisfy her curiosity, she succeeds in slipping through the looking glass and there she finds a world every bit as exciting and bizarre as Wonderland.

Mirrors, with their ability to reflect and distort the external environment have been regarded as instruments of magic from time to time. We are drawn to them and they seem to capture us. They reveal to us much about ourselves, yet what they reflect, like everything else, is subject to the screening operations of our visual/perceptual system. We may or may not really see what is in the mirror.

Imagery techniques permit us to slip through the looking-glass along with Alice and to meet the person who stares back at us. Looking-glass House is the place where our private eye can make contact with the person we project ourselves to be.

There are many special emphases which can be given to self imaging procedures but the overriding mission of all of them is basically the same. The goal is to get to know ourselves fully so that we might more understand, accept and love ourselves fully.

An essential aspect of our identity is the picture of ourselves which we carry in our heads at all times - our self image. Like all images, it is subject to the many distortions of which our psychoperceptual system is capable.

In healthy individuals, such distortion may be minimal. In those with severe mental, physical or social problems, it is likely to be maximal, and can function pathologically as either cause or effect. In any case, there is hardly anyone who cannot benefit from some therapeutic work with this Looking-glass Self.

Our self image is a powerful determinant of how we function in the world and how we feel about our selves and others. The more closely it approximates who and what we really are, the more it facilitates our being and doing. The greater its discrepancy with who and what we think we are or should be, the more problematical it becomes in our lives.

The purpose of a confrontation between our private eye and our Looking-glass Self is to provide an opporunity to determine the degree of clarity with which we view ourselves. Our need is to *see* ourselves clearly so that we become the world's greatest authority on our selves.

Given a face to face encounter with this projected self, Sherlock can discover, through dialogue, unfounded perceptions of inferiority and inadequacy along with unwarranted pretentions of superiority. Where actual physical weakness exists, the client can begin to incorporate and work with it rather than deal with it through denial and self rejection. If the impairment is emotional, the client will be deprived of her usual avoidance defenses in the self encounter and will have to explore the nature of her Depressed Self, Anxious Self, etc.

The technique is extraordinarily effective with problems in which the self image is an intrinsic issue, such as obesity; many sexual disorders; disfigurements from accidents, disease or surgery; developmental concerns, as in adolescence; extreme social self consciousness; etc. Such clients are often surprised to discover how negative their self image really is.

Out of work with the Looking-glass Self, the concept of the Best Self naturally evolves, providing the client with yet another therapeutic image that has healing potential. More will be said about this later.

When used as a general imagery technique, the procedure of encountering the Looking-glass Self is as follows. The person working alone will have to put the instructions on tape or have them committed to memory before beginning the exercise.

1. Pre-imagery relaxation.
2. The client is instructed to look at himself in an imaginary mirror and to describe what he sees in detail.
3. The therapist asks questions to ensure that the client has a clear image and to note if there is any difficulty with any

part of the body. The client is asked for information regarding how the image is clothed, what colors are apparent, what facial expression is observed, whether the image is stationary or in motion, what the hands are doing, the position of the feet, any background visualized, etc. The client is asked if he would recognize the image as himself if it was met on the street. Find out how it is different from the client.

4. The suggestion is given for the client to enter into dialogue with the image, to inquire about what life is like on the other side of the mirror. What is the emotional state of the Looking-glass Self? Why does it feel as it does? What does it think and feel about the client? What does it want for and of the client? Is it loving, friendly or hostile toward the client? Why does it feel as it feels about the client? Can it be of help to the client? Can the client be of help to it?

5. If there is vagueness regarding the above issues or if the Looking-glass Self is uncooperative, the client is invited to become the image and to experience it from the inside.

6. If there is further work to be done, a date is made for the next encounter. The client thanks and says good-bye to the Looking-glass Self.

7. When the image is gone, the client is invited to return to normal consciousness for a follow-up discussion of the experience. A drawing of the image may also be done as part of the follow-up.

8. An important variation to be considered when the imagery is therapeutically directed toward a sexual problem, a specific physical impairment or deformity, or feelings of physical inferiority or inadequacy is to have the client visualize himself nude. The rest of the procedure is essentially the same, except for questions about clothing.

9. If the client is unwilling or unable to Self image, suggest that he allow an image of something symbolizing the Self to appear and proceed as above.

The Case of the Girl in the Fun-House Mirror

Colleen's experience with this type of imagery is a good example of its effectiveness. At age twenty-seven, she came to therapy quite depressed having arrived at the conclusion there was nothing o.k. about her. She felt ugly, socially inept, sexually deficient, weird in her thoughts and feelings and unliked by everyone.

We visited Looking-glass House during her fifth therapy session. She found it difficult to get her Looking-glass Self in focus. She would get a glimpse, become uncomfortable and lose it. We patiently tried again and again.

Finally, Colleen was in touch. She described her mirror counterpart as grotesquely fat (Colleen was, perhaps, fifteen pounds overweight) with dwarf-like disproportions (she was short but well proportioned) and an especially prominent rear end (hers was not so large as to be an object of attention).

It was as if Colleen was looking into one of those Fun-House mirrors which allow us to recognize ourselves but reflects an image which is grossly distorted. As she gazed at the person in the mirror her facial expression registered disgust.

The Looking-glass Self sat huddled and withdrawn. She wore unfashionable clothes of drab colors (as did Colleen) and bore an expression of unfriendly apathy (also true of Colleen). The patient's first remark after describing this person was that she did not wish to approach her and did not think the person wanted to be approached.

"It's definitely me," said the client, "I'd know her anywhere." There was a contemptuous indifference in her voice and manner as she beheld this pathetic projection of herself.

It took some prodding to get Colleen involved in dialogue with this image whom she named "Downy." She was finally persuaded to ask Downy why she was so depressed. The unexpected answer came immediately, jarring both patient and therapist.

"Because of you, you two-faced, lying ass bitch!" screamed Downy. Colleen was obviously taken aback but could not control Downy's verbal stream.

"This is a shit hole of a prison behind the mirror," Downy continued, "and do you know why? Because there's nothing back here but what you're willing to give me and you're too stingy and scared to give me anything that's good."

Colleen appeared stunned but rose to her own defense. "I don't have anything to give you. You're a reflection of all that I am."

"Like hell!" came the retort. "You hide behind me. You're smart, you write poetry...You're compassionate...and there is even some prettiness in you...but you won't allow me to reflect any of that."

Colleen fell silent and a tear streaked across her cheek. "Is she right?" I inquired.

"She has no right to say that stuff." The patient's tone was angry but subdued.

I pressed. "But is she right?"

"Yes."

In just a few minutes the encounter with Downy had brought forth valuable material for therapeutic work. The Looking-glass Self was an angry, aggressive component of Colleen's personality that had been largely disowned.

The image immediately "spilled the beans" regarding the defensive function of the patient's negative self image and depression. The door was opened to an investigation of the reasons behind Colleen's playing down her postive attributes while exaggerating negative ones.

In follow-up, Colleen said she never wanted to make contact with Downy again. This became our therapeutic focus for a time, my position being that avoiding Downy was avoiding a part of herself and that she could never feel complete by doing that. She needed to accept and embrace Downy as a potential helper rather than an enemy.

Tentatively, the young woman resumed dialogue with her imaged Looking-glass Self. The image remained explicit regarding what she wanted from Colleen.

As a gesture of good will toward her, the patient tried dressing with a bit more style and color and wearing light makeup. They began to discuss their shared interest in poetry and the mutual satisfaction they could derive from helping others.

At the same time, Colleen and I were looking into the dynamics of her "need" to be the depressed, unattractive and unfriendly person she said she hated being. She started to be aware that this was a protection against establishing intimacy with other human beings. Her fears of being close outweighed her longing for it and, in the persona of Downy, she remained unapproachable and safe.

At a significant point in treatment, Downy protested that she did not like her name. The patient reassured her and surprised me by responding that the name no longer signified "a downer" as it had in the beginning. She now saw Downy as someone soft and comforting, like a downy pillow. In that context, the woman in the looking-glass was delighted to keep her name and the two of them were on their way to respecting and accepting each other.

In the process of Self imagery, negotiations for behavioral and attitudinal changes are being carried on between the client and another part of her nervous system projected imaginally. Ambivalence toward change is acted out and resolved in the dialogue between these two parts. In this case, changes such as dressing better, wearing make-up and acknowledging creativity were accomplished relatively quickly and easily.

Part of the therapeutic power of imagery lies in the fact that such changes are negotiated without direct involvement of the therapist. The client does not enter into some kind of implicit or explicit contract for change with the therapist. The contracting is done directly between aspects of the client's personality which are in conflict. The problems inherent in the client's doing things to please the therapist are minimized.

The Case of the Missing Part

Another young woman named Lois imaged most of her body in a positive light. She had come to therapy because she had never experienced orgasm in her relations with her husband.

Lois encountered her Looking-glass Self in the nude and described the various parts of her body in a wholesome, straightforward way until she got to her genital area. There, she found her visualization blurred, as if an airbrush had been used to remove detail from a photograph.

She initiated dialogue with her vagina-less self who said, "You don't really want to see what's between my legs." At that point, Lois became overtly anxious and asked to stop the imagery. I asked only that she agree to meet her Looking-glass Self at another time before returning quickly to ordinary consciousness.

In our follow-up she said she understood exactly what the image meant and that it had shaken her. It was pointing out to her the issue she was most reluctant yet most needed to deal with. Since I was completely in the dark, I asked her to elucidate.

"When I was in college," she explained, "I was on the volley ball team—a pretty good player. Our assistant coach was one of the gym teachers. She had only been out of school for just a few years and was absolutely beautiful. She was tall with an athletic build and stunning red hair. After she and I had became good friends, she confided that she was gay.

"I thought she was wonderful and could have cared less. I had never been very intense about sex. At that point, I had had relations with two different guys but didn't find it very exciting with either of them. I was totally oblivious to the attraction I felt toward Steffie and saw myself as an enlightened, broad minded person who could certainly have a lesbian for a friend.

"Then, one night after Steffie and I had enjoyed an elegant meal with wine and lots of intimate conversation, we returned to her place and she seduced me. I mean, I was willing enough but she did apply some pressure. As our embraces got more heated I told myself it was just an experiment which I would probably do once and forget.

"Then, something happened which I would never have dreamed of. I went absolutely wild with passion. I never knew I could get so turned on. It was great.

"For about a year we couldn't get enough of each other. It ended when she got a job at another school and left town.

"I was heartbroken. We corresponded for a while but she soon started living with someone and stopped writing.

"Missing her was bad enough but the experience left me totally convinced I was a lesbian. I concluded I'd never be able to relate to a man again.

"The weird thing is that I started to think of myself as a very masculine person although I know I'm really not. My attraction to other females became an obsession with me. I didn't act on my feelings but all of my fantasies were built around them.

"At one point, I got this crazy idea that I was probably growing a penis. As wild as it sounds, it actually worried me a lot. I got to thinking I'd better not look at my genitals or I might actually see a penis there.

"When Dan came into my life, he was so thoughtful and attentive that I knew I wanted to marry him. We both wanted to put off having intercourse until we were married so I was able to convince myself that there wasn't going to be any problem.

"I thought my love for him would take care of my sexual doubts and I guess it has mentally but I can't respond to him physically. I get nervous when he enters me and lose any feeling of arousal. I guess deep down I'm still convinced I'm gay.

"I finally broke down and told him about Steffie and he was real understanding about it. That's when he suggested I get some help."

No doubt all of this would have unfolded during the process of conventional therapy but imagery brought Lois' basic problem quickly into focus and also provided a framework for intervention via further confrontation with her Looking-glass Self.

In subsequent encounters, Lois came to recognize that she was dealing with an image of her masculine self. She allowed herself to look sharply at the genital area and found there was, as she had feared, a penis there.

It took some time for her to feel o.k. about that. Her early life learning had convinced her that a human being is an either/or—either masculine or feminine. It was a revelation for her to think about all males having a feminine self and all females a masculine self but the concept made sense to her and helped her to put her Looking-glass Self into perspective.

She acknowledged to herself that there was a strong, masculine component of her personality but was convinced that this need not in any way inhibit her being female and feminine. She discovered that she could direct her masculine traits into productive channels in her career field and some of her recreational activities while being a receptive female in the bedroom. Following a course of sex therapy, she and her husband reported that they had achieved a mutually satisfying sexual relationship.

Working With The Best Self

A useful variation on the Looking-glass Self is the Best Self. This technique involves having clients visualize not the person they perceive themselves to be at the moment but the person they are striving to become. It goes as follows:

"Now that you're relaxed, allow yourself to get in touch with an image of the person you are becoming. See yourself not only as you want to be physically, but also with the kind of outlook and attitude you most desire to have. See yourself as the person who relates to others the way you really want to. Get in touch with your Best Self—you at your fullest potential. When you have that image before you, please describe it to me."

Following these instructions, the procedure is the same as for the Looking-glass Self. The patient is invited into dialogue with the image and can often get information and advice on how to accelerate the process of becoming her Best Self.

It is particularly meaningful to have the client become the Best Self and to experience how it feels to be in that mode. Many clients are profoundly struck by the way the Best Self feels and experiences things in contrast to how they feel and experience things in the present. Usually they report a remarkable sense of well being when they become their Best Self.

In the follow-up, it is generally helpful to inform clients that we all have a natural tendency to grow in a healthy direction and that this process goes on to some degree no matter what our current problems are. Therefore, The Best Self is not someone they have to go out and find. It is already enfolded within them, waiting for the opportunity to emerge.

That opportunity can be enhanced by addressing the problematical issues in their lives and proceeding to grow psychologically and spiritually but they do not have to incorporate anything essentially new. The seed for all that they can become was already planted long ago and awaits fruition.

From the Therapist's Notebook:
Me and My Shadow

I sit beside the pond and invite my Best Self to appear. Immediately he is there standing in the bright sunlight. He is smiling and relaxed, enjoying the surroundings.

I take some time to scrutinize him carefully. I am looking for differences between us. Except for the fact that he is a little slimmer I can find nothing.

My ego swells. Am I that close to self actualization? Good for me!

I get up from my place in the shade and walk out into the sunlight to greet Best Self. He is friendly as I approach.

"You know what?," I said excitedly. " I was just comparing the two of us and the only major difference I can find is a few pounds. We're getting pretty close, old buddy.

"Not really." Best Self continues to smile.

I am taken aback. "What? What do you mean?"

He points to the ground and I am aware of his shadow. It is very short and narrow.

Then, I notice my own shadow. Though the two of us are standing in exactly the same light mine is broad and extends far beyond his.

I am dismayed by the pointedness of the lesson but accept its validity. My Best Self has integrated much of his dark side. He has made conscious and accepted his Shadow.

I on the other hand have much work to do. There is still much of myself that I attempt to disown. Best Self reminds me that I am in the process of becoming what he is. He promises to help me.

CHAPTER NINE

SEEING RED AND OTHER COLORS

Color is a vital element of our lives. It permeates our language. If we're not seeing red, we might be crying the blues or feeling green with envy. A coward may be yellow to the core, a villain may have a black heart and a healthy person may be in the pink.

We experience some colors as sensuous, others as exciting and others as repulsive. We reveal something about our moods and personalities in the colors we select for our clothing, furnishings and automobiles. Color is especially expressive of feeling states.

Color seems to have the power to disturb or soothe, to promote dis-ease or healing. Lawrence Blair (1976) in his *Rhythms of Vision*, cites examples of scientific work revealing that certain colors can go beyond merely arousing a particular mood and can, in fact, have a measurable physiological impact on the body. Obviously, important applications of such information are possible in the selection of colors for medical and psychiatric facilities, schools and the workplace in general.

The notion of color having healing properties is not at all new. The ancient Indian approach to healing known as Ayurvedic Medicine teaches that the basic seven colors of the rainbow are related to the tissues of the body and are instrumental in maintaining the balance of the three bodily humors or tridosha. A modern Ayurvedic text by Dr. Vasant Lad (1984), prescribes wrapping a piece of gelatinous paper of any of the basic colors around a jar of water, placing it in the sunlight for four hours allowing the water to become infused with the vibrations of the color and, then, drinking it for certain beneficial results.

As in all things, there are many differences in how specific individuals perceive and are affected by colors but some generalizations apply. Red, for example, is generally a highly stimulating color. It connotes fire, blood, heat and excitement. It is the color of deep passion and desire. Liturgically, it symbolizes the Holy Spirit who "fires up" the Christian's heart. Patriotically, it symbolizes the blood of fallen heroes. It is the color of action and reaction at a fever pitch.

Orange is a shade less intense than red but retains much of its excitement. Lying as it does between red and yellow, which is symbolic of intellectual illumination, orange is the more controlled and subdued expression of all that red stands for. It suggests ambition and self seeking more than primitive passion.

Yellow generally brings to mind light, lightness and enlightenment. It is the color associated with the sun, the source of life and all its satisfactions. It connotes brightness and cheerfulness.

Nearly everyone associates green with the earth and vegetation. It is the color of growth and fertility. Green symbolizes nature and abundance. In more materialistic persons, it may symbolize money and security.

Blue is the color of the sky and the ocean. It represents the heights and depths of feeling. It can bring to mind the unbounded freedom of the heavens and the exaltation of the spirit. It can also represent the murky depths of the psyche and descent into the underworld. Generally it is a color perceived as soothing and cooling.

Purple is popularly associated with royalty, stateliness, order and power. It signifies maximum achievement and self realization in the worldly sense.

Just as purple suggests the heights of earthly accomplishment, the color just beyond it, violet, suggests advanced spirituality. It is the color of healing, reconciliation and forgiveness. It connotes transcendence, going beyond the boundaries of space, time, energy and matter.

Imaging Through the Rainbow

Allowing for a host of idiosyncratic interpretations of the various colors, one can make use of them in a variety of therapeutic imagery techniques. The one I am about to describe is especially productive with emotionally constricted patients. The inherent link between colors and emotions elicits an outflow of feelings, providing a wealth of emotionally charged images any or all of which can be worked with in ensuing psychotherapy sessions.

Fundamentally, the mission calls for the private eye to encounter the seven basic colors, allow them to take a form and to do something with that form. The instructions I use proceed as follows:

> Now that you're relaxed, I invite you to get in touch with an image of the color red—just the color. Take your time and, if you have difficulty, let me know but allow the sensation of "red" to enter your mind's eye.
> (Client reports contact with the color.)
> Make full contact with the red. Let it envelope you and tell me what feelings, if any, you are aware of.
> (Client reports feelings.)
> Now allow your red to take some form, any form - it doesn't have to be anything that is traditionally red. It doesn't have to make any sense. Just let it take whatever form it wants and, then, describe it to me.
> (Client describes a red "something.")
> Please move closer to the "something" and tell me what you feel as you approach it.
> (Client reports feelings.)
> Now please think about what you would like to do with or about your "something" and tell me what that is.
> (We discuss what the client would like to do. If it is anti-therapeutic such as "destroy it," I ask him to tell the "something" what he feels like doing but to not actually do it. The "something" is then asked to respond to the feelings expressed and the client and object continue to dialogue.
> If the desired action is not anti-therapeutic, such as "touch it," I encourage the client to carry out the action and, then, initiate dialogue with the object. When closure is reached, I instruct him to let go of the "something" for the time being and proceed to the next color, following the same format.)

Anyone working alone on this exercise will do best to memorize the format so that she can move fluidly from one sequence to the next. Recording the experience in a journal for subsequent review can replace the follow-up portion of the procedure.

There should be no push to cram all seven colors into a single session. On many occasions, I have spent the entire session working with one color. There have been times when a single color provided enough therapeutic grist to keep the mill turning for several sessions. As always, time should be left for a follow-up before the session ends.

When a client pleads difficulty in visualizing pure color, it is sometimes expeditious to move on to the next step and instruct, "O.K., then just image something that is that color." You will need to get this peson involved in giving a lot of detail about her image.

Defensive, rigid and compulsive clients are usually quite guarded imaginally, producing such stereotypes as a red ball, an orange orange, a yellow lemon, etc. The step of having the client do something with the object makes it possible for the therapist to help him get beyond the stereotypical form by manipulating and having dialogue with it. It is difficult to stay within the safe confines a red apple provides if you are talking with it, ingesting it or allowing it to grow to the size of a building.

Joanne was a "please everybody" person. In interpersonal relationships, she was passive and compliant. She decided what to do on the basis of how other people would feel about it and was frequently exploited but wouldn't voice any complaints. She swallowed large portions of anger every day on the grounds that expressing it might alienate one of her significant others.

When asked to image red, Joanne could only come up with a rather washed out version of it. Enveloped in it, she said she felt "sick." Her red took the form of an overripe tomato, soft and squishy.

In follow-up, she was able to relate this image to her internalized angry, aggressive feelings which she keeps stored up until they rot. She liked to think that her anger was soft and harmless like the tomato.

This woman wanted to bury her tomato. I insisted that she mark the spot so she could return and exhume it at a later date. Of course, she followed my directions to a T.

Following a productive period of psychotherapy, Joanne went back for her tomato as we had agreed she would. At this time, however, she had it in mind to throw it at a particularly toxic person in her life. She imaged it splattering in her target's face and felt marked satisfaction.

On the reality level, she soon after had a confrontation with this same nemesis. During their exchange, she was firm and assertive and walked away feeling like a winner.

Another female patient, Irene, was emotionally scarred by growing up in a home with four brothers and a tyrannical father. She and her mother were totally oppressed by the males in the family. She had an I.Q. near 140 but had completed only high school and was married to a man intellectually and socially inferior who abused her physically.

Like Joanne, Irene tended to avoid the aggressive under-pinnings of red and orange. When she got to yellow, the color of enlightenment, she was uplifted. It took the form of a beautiful dress in the window of a store. She looked at it adoringly but averred that she could not afford to buy it and would have to leave it there.

Her image was true to her character. The dress, like her wonderful intellect and the bright side of her personality had to be disowned.

I got her involved in a dialogue with the shopkeeper, an older woman resembling her grandmother (the only nurturing person in Irene's life). They negotiated an agreement that the dress would be held for the duration of, at least, three more therapy sessions. I banked on the possibility that the patient would feel more deserving of the dress at that time and would find some way to claim it.

Those sessions were devoted to having Irene give herself permission to be the smart, capable person she is. She had much fear about presenting herself to be superior to any male in any way.

The males in her family had always squelched any effort on her part to act their equal. Her husband had taken up where they left off. She was utterly surprised to find me, another male, encouraging her to be more assertive.

As I had hoped, she returned in fantasy to the dress shop and tried on the dress. With encouragement, she entertained more and more imagery of herself in the dress. Simultaneously, she began to display more assertiveness and self confidence.

Green turned out to be a breakthrough color for Marshall an engineer who was compulsive, precise and totally committed to rationality. He came to therapy because his wife was extremely dissatisfied with his limited capacity for communicating about feeling issues. He acknowledged his limitation but negated the value of feelings in the first place.

Predictably, Marshall exhibited strong resistance to imagery but finally decided to give it a try. The color mission was his very first experience with it.

This patient came up with a red telephone which he identified as the hot line over which the U.S. and Russia would negotiate either's decision to nuke the world. I filed this as a suggestion of how much hostility he was carrying around inside.

His orange was a plastic paperweight and his yellow was a flower. Then, when he got to green, something broke loose which he almost managed to censor.

I observed him closely as he allowed himself to be enveloped in green, reporting no feeling awareness, just as he had with the previous colors. I asked him to let the green take form and, for just an instant, he snickered.

"What was that?" I asked quickly.

"Nothing," he replied, resuming a sober countenance.

"There was something that amused you. Now, you're censoring it."

"It was stupid and impossible," he said with irritation.

"Marshall, your inner world is full of things that are stupid and impossible in the outer world. That's why you're visiting it - don't let your left brain scoff it off."

There was a long pause before he said tersely, "It was a green giraffe."

Right away, I felt some hope for Marshall and it turned out that his green giraffe became his guide to the world of emotions in subsequent sessions. Today, he remains basically rigid and solidly surrounded by rational defenses but he has learned enough from Beanstalk, the giraffe, to engage in more feeling exchanges with his wife, leaving her more content and their relationship improved.

Many clients have reported sensations of flying or floating when engulfed in blue. Blue is the gate to the deepest or highest (depending on your perspective) part of the color / feeling spectrum. The colors that follow it suggest transcendence of earthly passions.

Beth, who was overly reactive emotionally, was a sensitive, feeling person who had not developed adquate defenses to keep her feelings in check. Just as she was capable of pouring forth love and affection, she was equally capable, under stress, of releasing torrents of rage.

On her color mission, she discoverd a lovely, purple butterfly. It guided her to a garden where each kind of flower represented a specific emotion. It proceeded to show her that it was possible to sip a little from each without becoming engorged.

In dialogue, the butterfly informed her that it was the monarch of the garden. It offered to help her learn how to be the monarch of her feelings.

Beth's experience is commonplace in imagery work. On almost every color mission, the patient encounters one or more symbols with which they can do further work. It is fascinating to watch this process and to see how much wisdom these symbols communicate. This, of course, is wisdom that has been enfolded within the client all along.

One of the most impressive effects of color imagery I have observed occurred a few years ago with a woman named Molly who was struggling desperately to come to terms with the incestuous abuse she had received during childhood. She could not seem to let go of the rage she felt toward her father who was dead and unavailable for the confrontational encounter for which she longed. She acheived some release by dialoguing with an image of her father but remained in extreme emotional turmoil.

When we sent her private eye on the color mission, red became her father's blood pouring from wounds she had inflicted on him. As the exercise progressed, however, she reported an increasing sense of peace that seemed very strange to her.

Engulfed in blue, she felt herself detaching from all of her past pain. She visualized a blue kite soaring higher and higher into the sky. It was carrying all of her suffering away with it. She watched until it faded completely out of sight.

Molly's purple became a purple robe, connoting royalty. As she put it on she verbally acknowledged being a princess; a good, worthwhile human being. She felt she was rejoining the human race.

By the time she enveloped herself in violet, the patient felt a great burden being lifted from her. The violet became an elixir in a silver chalice and she wished fervently to drink it. As she swallowed the last of it, she said, "All is forgiven."

In our follow-up, Molly said she knew at the moment she drank from the cup that she had truly forgiven her father. I was somewhat skeptical but her behavior and attitude reflected definite changes thereafter.

There was no evidence of anything having been repressed. She seemed to have truly dropped her burden of hate and blame and was able to go on and address other problems in her life. She acknowledged and conveyed a serenity she had never known before. It appeared that the imagery was instrumental in accomplishing this.

A part of me says she was ready to let go anyway and the imagery simply marked the passage. Another part of me says she truly drank a healing potion concocted in a separate reality where the laws of the universe do not apply. While I debate the issues, the patient continues to reflect a dramatic improvement and that's pretty miraculous no matter what the cause.

From the Therapist's Notebook: Drowning

I have a few minutes between appointments. I am aware of feeling tense but cannot connect the tension with anything.

I close my eyes and make no effort to direct my imagery. Whatever comes will teach me something.

The color blue invades my visual field. It is a hard, cold, dark blue, not like the bright blue which lifts me up into the sky. My skin grows cold. I have a sensation of being in deep water.

I am numbed and frightened. I want to swim to the surface

but something is trying to pull me down. I do not want to remain in this blue abyss.

I hold my breath and thrust to the surface. Just as I break through my eyes pop open.

I am momentarily puzzled, somewhat disoriented. I wonder where that image came from. I check my calendar to reorient. It is then that I see the name of my next client and am enlightened.

It is the name of a woman who is young but badly broken. Her level of depression frequently frightens me. She tends to become extremely self destructive. I fear she has no more reserves. The next thing that goes wrong in her life may be the last thing she will tolerate.

My imagery tells me that I am allowing myself to be drawn into the vortex of her depression. My fear is that I will drown in her feelings just as she is drowning in them.

Why am I so vulnerable to her emotional state?

Feelings drift to the surface. I am tired. There has been too much recent loss in my life. I too am unsure I can bear yet another burden. My client hooks into that part of me which wants to abandon the journey. My fears are as much for me as they are for her.

I put my thoughts aside and take a deep breath. I close my eyes and leave everything outside of myself behind. I feel a downward movement as I withdraw to within myself. My body relaxes.

I envision a white light flickering internally, about midpoint in my abdomen. I focus on it and it brightens. With each breath I imagine that I am breathing life into the light.

After a few breaths the light brightens; a few more and it flares. I feel its warmth as it starts to spread upward into my chest and downward into my loins. It continues to get brighter and warmer as it fills my entire inner space.

Now I see it overflowing, radiating outwardly. It surrounds my body. I am enveloped in this healing, protective white light.

I return to ordinary consciousness feeling completely safe. I continue to sense the light around me like a force field.

I am able to work well with my very sick client. During our session she comments that she feels more and more depleted as she listens to herself.

She observes that most others in her life seem to be "pulled down" by her. She wonders how I remain so energized when I am with her.

"I'll teach you how I do it," I say.

She says she would like that. I suggest that she breathe deeply and allow her eyes to close.

As she relaxes I say, "Now imagine a ball of white light inside of you, about the middle of your body..........

CHAPTER TEN

LAND OF
WONDERS

Every human being dreams. The universal phenomenon of dreaming has captured man's attention since antiquity.

The mystery of dreams has never been solved despite all of our advances in science and technology. Much has been learned about the how of dreaming—the neurophysiological process. We know that it accompanies the REM (Rapid Eye Movement) stage of sleep which recurs at roughly ninety minute intervals during the sleep period but we don't know why we dream or why dreams take the particular form they do.

Some say that dreams are meaningless neurological discharges of conscious residue while others contend that they are significant messages from our unconscious minds. It is hard to dispute that they are products of the unconscious because they do, in fact, occur when we are "out like a light."

During our dreams, we experience ourselves as being awake even though we are asleep. We find ourselves in a strange realm where past, present and future seem to flow freely into each other.

We visit places and landscapes which seem entirely familiar and others which are unearthly and alien. We meet both the living and dead, all of whom seem equally alive. We meet people we know, people we don't know and people we know, yet don't know.

We find ourselves and others involved in carrying out some actions which are characteristic of us and some which are totally foreign. We run the gamut of experience from utter horror to ecstatic joy. We violate the laws of physics, society and God with varying degrees of impunity. We suffer physically, emotionally, and even die.

Life in dreamland is consummately complete albeit a little wild and crazy. Of course, if we took that life as the norm, we should have to consider our waking life to be madness. Dreamland is a land of wonders filled with images which are every bit as vivid and real to us as those filtered through our waking psychoperceptual system.

When we consciously and deliberately image, we are aware that we are making use of our imagination, whatever that is, but what is happening when we dream? We are not consciously and deliberately calling up images—they are spontaneous, uninvited. In this instance, is our imagination making use of us? Where do the images come from?

Convincing but differing answers can be found in the work of the two cornerstones of psychiatry, Freud and Jung. It was Freud's contention that the Ego (the conscious self) relegates to the unconscious unpleasant desires, memories and ideas which come to it during our waking periods.

During sleep, when the Ego is decommisioned and no longer vigilant, this repressed material surfaces in the context of dreams. The material is disguised (symbolized) to make it less disturbing and, thus, to preserve sleep. The father of psychoanalysis believed that much of the repressed material was related to sexual thoughts and feelings.

In Freud's system, dreams are biologically rooted guardians of sleep whose content is built on the residue of conscious material which threatens us in some way. By decoding them, we can better understand our neurotic conflicts and our unconscious wishes and drives.

In contrast, Jung professed that the unconscious is more than just a reservoir for the unwelcome components of our thinking/feeling experience. He posited that our personal unconscious fulfills that function but that we also have a collective unconscious. This is the storehouse of thinking/feeling processes inherited from our ancestral past which includes the entire history of our species and our animal ancestry as well. It is the wellspring of the accumulated wisdom of the ages.

Given this added dimension to the concept of unconsciousness, Jung's view is that. beyond merely processing repressed material, dreams compensate for the limited comprehension of our waking egos. In his system, dreams have a very positive function in that they can point to ways in which the dreamer might solve problems, grow and be enriched.

Jung looked upon dream symbols as reflections of religious and mythic as well as sexual ideation. He attached particular significance to archetypal dream symbols, an archetype being an emotionally charged universal thought form which corresponds to something of significance in one's conscious, waking life. It is a preformed conception of something that partially determines how that something will be perceived. The archetype of mother, for example, produces an image of a mother figure which is identified with the actual mother.

Those who follow Freud view dream images strictly as reflections of what lies in the basement of our neuropsychological system. Proponents of Jung see them as messengers from a realm which transcends time and space. As such, they are qualified to instruct and guide us. Both men would agree that dreaming serves a function mysteriously necessary to our psychological health.

Of course, there are other approaches to understanding dream imagery. In addition to scientific studies of dreams, there are numerous religious and occult traditions which adhere to their own interpretation of dream material.

In Pursuit of the Dream

When we send our private eye on a mission into dreamland, we must expect encounters with the unknown, unexpected, even the bizarre. We find ourselves in a land of wonder, much as Lewis Carroll's Alice did when she pursued a bunny down a rabbit hole. This excursion, by the way, turned out to be a dream just as was her visit to Looking-glass House.

As we pursue the lessons of our dreams, we must, like Alice, adapt ourselves to the impossible for that is the substance of the terrain. We must be prepared to talk with plants and animals and inanimate things.

The flora and fauna of dreamland are not that of the material universe. There are unclassified species to be met and unearthly geographies to be mapped. We become explorers and adventurers not in search of conquest but of enlightenment.

Techniques for working with dream imagery are as limitless as the imagination. Many variations on the approach I describe here are possible. The basic mission is to have the private eye track down and fully encounter a dream image which, in the dreamer's opinion, is particularly interesting, instructive, frightening, puzzling, etc.

The encounter may take place within the framework of the dream, meaning that the client returns to dreamland and meets the image on its own turf. Optionally, the image may be brought into the client's immediate environment (the therapist's office, for example) and confronted there.

I encourage a return to dreamland if the dream seems especially vague or confusing or lacks closure. If the patient has a sense of having integrated the dream as a whole but wants more involvement with a particular dream image, an encounter in the here and now might be preferred. Occasionally a patient is scared of the dream material to the extent that he feels unwilling or unable to return to it and this would be strong justification for bringing the dream image to the patient's turf rather than vice versa.

The Case of the Deadly Wings

The procedure is best demonstrated by a verbatim account. The excerpt which follows is taken from my work with a twenty-seven year old male social worker who came to therapy seeking to resolve his bisexual orientation in one direction or the other. He was then dating a female colleague and had developed a caring relationship with her which was closer than any previous relationship with a woman.

This client, Brent, had grown up in complete awe of his father who was affluent, handsome, cultured, and fearsome when annoyed. In earlier dreams, the father appeared with god-like status, in total control of everything, including Brent.

There had been frankly sexual dreams in which the patient gratefully received his father's penis into his mouth. In these dreams, Brent felt more a sense of exaltation than arousal. He likened it to taking all of his father's considerable charm and power into himself.

On a conscious level, this patient could articulate that his father was not perfect but he could not bring himself to make negative statements of a specific nature about him. He seemed to be saying, "Intellectually I don't buy the concept of perfection but I can't find any flaws in my dad."

As we were focusing on the father/son relationship, Brent brought in a dream which he said included an image he wanted to work with. I invited him to relax, to go back to the dream place, and to recount the dream in the present tense as if it were happening right now.

"I am in the presence of an older man who is calculating, grotesque and hateful. I am repulsed by him, but he gets me very excited by telling me he can give me the power to fly.

"I want desperately to fly to Europe and tell him I will accept his gift. He says there will be one condition—that I will have to put a liquid explosive, wrapped in plastic envelopes, into my breast and pants pockets. He tells me they will explode eventually—by his free will or if I turn against him.

"I am anxious to get going and am now airborne. I have a terrible feeling in my gut that the explosives will go off at any minute but I still want to go to Europe.

"As my flight continues the fear becomes overwhelming. I cannot continue. I return to this country and take the explosives out of my pocket."

T: What are you feeling?

B: (Visibly shaken) Scared.

T: What particular element of the dream do you wish to work with?

B: The old man. I feel there is something unfinished between us.

T: Very well. Do you want to meet him in the land of your dream or back here?

B: Here.

T: In that case, allow yourself to gradually return to these surroundings and, when you feel completely here, let me know.

(Pause.)

B: O.K., I'm back.

T: Now, would you bring the old man here and put him somewhere where you can look him over?

B: He's on the sofa in the corner. He's truly ugly. He has lumps, maybe cysts on his forehead and cheeks. He's dressed very plain - just black pants and a white shirt. His eyes are dark and piercing and his mouth is kind of curled on one side. He looks mean, cruel.

T: Will you find out if he has a name?

B: He says he is called Skymaster. He rules the heavens.

T: Ask him why he is in your dream and what he wants of you.

B: What do you want from me? (Pause) He's smiling at me. His mouth is hideous. His teeth look rotted. He says he wants to share his powers with me.

T: Tell him your response to that.

B: I don't believe you. You scare me. I think you really want to kill me. (Pause) He says, "Would a father try to kill his son?" (Pause) You're not my father! (Long pause)

T: What are you experiencing?

B: He says, "Don't be too sure."

T: What do you say?

B: My father is handsome and brilliant. He wants me to be successful like he is. You offer me wings but they

carry with them the seeds of my destruction. (Pause) Skymaster says that's to insure that I never, never become as powerful as he is. He will accept me only as long as I am weaker than he—he wants me to be subservient to him.
T: So, what will you do about the deal he is offering?

B: I see now that it's no deal at all. The idea of possessing his magic is very seductive but he's not really going to let me do that. He's going to remain in control no matter what powers I get from him. (Pause) You can keep your wings, Skymaster. Only, now, I'm not going to be disappointed about being earthbound like I was in the dream. I'll learn to fly on my own.

T: How does he receive that?

B: He's just glaring at me but I feel stronger now. I feel in control.

T: Are you ready to let him go?

B: Yes.

T: Then do so and, when you are ready, open your eyes.

Brent opened his eyes and raised his hand, signaling that he wanted to be quietly reflective for a moment. I respected his need and waited for him to speak.

"Just as I opened my eyes," he said, "I remembered something from mythology. It was about a boy whose father gave him wings to fly and he crashed."

I informed him that I happened to know the story well.

"That's the myth about Daedalus," I said. "He was a famous builder who fashioned a fantastic labyrinth for his king. Then, he fell into disfavor and the king imprisoned him in a tower along with his young son, Icarus.

"Daedalus concluded the only way he and Icarus could escape would be through the air. So he fashioned two sets of wings made of feathers held together by thread and wax. When they were completed, sure enough, he was able to fly.

"Just before departing from the tower, Daedalus told Icarus to maintain a moderate altitude because, if he flew too high, the sun might melt the wax on his wings. They took off together and were doing fine until the boy became exuberant and began to soar higher and higher. As predicted, the sun melted the wax holding the feathers together and Icarus plunged to his death in the sea."

Brent looked deeply thoughtful as he spoke. "It's basically the same thing as the dream. Icarus got too far above his father and was destroyed."

"Yes," I said, "but unlike Skymaster, Daedalus tried to prevent the boy's death and was deeply grieved."

"Right," said the patient. "Skymaster wasn't going to leave it up to natural powers like the sun. He was ready to blow me to bits."

"Is he your father?" I asked.

Brent pressed folded hands against his mouth for a few moments before speaking. "I'll have to think about that. If so, it's a part of my father I've never looked at before."

The richness of dream imagery is awesome. Were I a Carl Jung or Joseph Campbell, I'm sure I could have helped my client to do more impressive things with his imagery, but the beauty of it all is that Brent got plenty out of what we did with just my modest talents. It led to new insights about his father and their relationship.

The Case of the Dying Grass

Sometimes a dream image takes on a significant role in the patient's continuing therapy. Such was the case with an extremely passive, masochistic young woman named Dora who was addicted to abusive men and practically insisted that all of her friends exploit her.

It took Dora several therapy sessions before she could face how physically, mentally and spiritually depleted she was. I insisted that there were unexplored parts of herself that could enhance her recovery, if only she would search for them. She expressed disbelief until the following dream occurred:

> "The St. Augustine grass in my yard is dying and an agricultural expert who looks like you (the therapist) has come over to look at it. While you're doing this, a big, ferocious dog comes bounding up. I feel afraid of it, but it is friendly to me and I know, somehow, he belongs to me. I know that he has been way out in the woods with some other wild animals. I am afraid that he wants to go join them, but he comes when I call him. At first, there is a glass wall between the dog and me but he finally comes around the wall. Just then, I notice that half of the grass is dead and half is alive."

Dora, who owned a cat and had never been around dogs worked closely with her imaged canine who identified himself as Yippie. He pointed out that being passive and saintly (symbolized by the grass) was killing her.

Yippie said he had been sent to guide her into the wilds so that she could learn from creatures who were less tame than she. He introduced her to a number of aggressive animals from whom she learned to be more assertive and less afraid of "primitive" feelings. Yippie has remained her Guide until this day.

Higher Consciousness in Dreams

Dream images are versatile in that they can teach lessons, promote healing, solve problems and do creative work. Great authors like Robert Louis Stevenson, William Blake, Samuel Taylor Coleridge and Edgar Alan Poe have acknowledged dream material to be the basis for some of their works.

Elias Howe, the inventor, got the design for the needle of his sewing machine from a dream. The Angel Gabriel first appeared to the prophet Mohammed in a dream. The chemist, Kekule, formulated the ring sturcture of benzine through a dream. The list could go on.

All of this supports the concept of dreams opening to us vistas of higher consciousness and creativity. Likewise, there is evidence to support telepathic and precognitive aspects of dreaming. Dream images have the power to transcend the material universe.

Elsie, a sensitive young woman with an exciting intellect was beginning to emerge from a severe depression when she had the following dream.

I am on the beach with some other people and we are involved in jumping. I am not doing as well as the others. Then, I see approaching a woman I have to describe as beautiful although she is not physically exceptional. She is tall and slender but most of all, I'm aware that she is a free soul. She comes up and talks to me and we laugh together. I feel relieved that she is there and kind of... well, more complete, like she is a part of me that has been missing. After we talk, I start jumping real high and I am able to stay in the air a long time.

Thus began Elsie's relationship with Eastre, her Higher Consciousness. The meeting signalled a reclaiming of her importance and power as a female. For the previously despondent patient it was an impressive rebirth.

Although Elsie was not conscious of the fact, it later came to light that the name Eastre designates the goddess of dawn whose annual festival at the vernal equinox was called Eastre.

Since the Christian Feast of the Resurrection occurred about the same time, the pagan name was borrowed for it when Christianity was introduced to England. The spelling was slightly changed.

From the Therapist's Notebook:

The dream was magnificent. I was traveling with Buddha in a conveyance resembling a horse drawn sleigh but there was no horse. The sleigh traveled swiftly on water like a boat.

Buddha and I were making the rounds of all the islands of Japan. We stopped at village after village and were well received by everyone. Each time we cast off for the next place the Buddha clanged a bell at the rear of the sleigh/boat.

Though I recall no details the travels were extensive and the dream long. Finally Buddha said we had visited all of the islands and clanged the bell for the last time as we headed home. I felt a mixture of deep satisfaction and sadness that our journey was ending.

The scene changed to a later time and I was walking the streets of a Japanese village looking for the home of Buddha. When I reached the house I found it had been preserved as an historic site.

One wall of the house was glass encased permitting me to look in at the pallette on which Buddha had lain at the time of his death.. It was a simple bed roll. On a small table beside it was a golden cup.

Although I had known Buddha was dead I experienced a sense of disappointment until I noticed an enjoining wall which was covered with rice paper. Behind the paper, visible only in silhouette, was our beloved sleigh/boat. Beside the vehicle, also in silhouette, was a life-size likeness of the Buddha, his right index finger pointing heavenward.

It was an unusually vivid dream which left me exhilirated. It's style was a departure from my usual pattern of dreaming. It seemed special and I wanted to do more with it.

In imagery I returned to the Japanese house and called for Buddha to come forth. He appeared in classical picture-book form, wearing a saffron robe and looking quite jolly.

I felt in awe as I thanked him for appearing and asked him why he had come into my dream. As I spoke I realized I had taken on the appearance and manner of a child.

Buddha extended his arms to me and picked me up as I ran to him.

"I am in your dream to reward you for your seeking of me," he said gently. His rotund body felt like a solid underpinning as he held me aloft.

"We travel together," he continued, "just as in the dream."

"It was a wonderful journey," I said, "but why did it have to end so sadly at your tomb?"

"Did you see Buddha in the tomb?" he asked.

"No. It was empty."

"Do you see Buddha alive now?"

"Yes."

"I brought you to the tomb to remind you that after the earthly journey is done there are still other places to go. At the tomb, which many suppose to be the final place, you discovered my shadow beside the shadow of our vehicle. I am pointing upward to show you I have transcended the things of the earth."

"I had hoped to find you at the house as I find you now," I said, confessing my disappointment in the dream.

Buddha set my feet back on the ground. I felt extremely small. He seemed to tower above me.

"You can find me as I am at any time. Study yourself to find me. Forget yourself to find me. It is my teaching that all living beings are Buddhas. The lesson is to forget what you think you are and find out what you really are."

Without the slightest warning he disappeared.

I am still pondering the lessons of the dream.

CHAPTER ELEVEN

UPON MY WORD

Words are wonderful inventions. With them, we are empowered to communicate our deepest feelings, to express the most abstract of concepts, to preserve our historical past and to explain and pass on the complexities of our scientific and technological operations.

Words can be mighty weapons which, under certain conditions, can hurt and even kill. Conversely, they can nurture, heal and transform as they convey tenderness, love, and wisdom.

Small wonder that, throughout the history of mankind, words have been regarded with a certain amount of awe and imbued with magical properties. Words are an essential part of our most solemn and sacred observances. They are the basis of all of our contractual transactions, pacts, treaties and proclamations.

When a person gives her word on something, that something becomes fully backed and binding. A man of his word is dependable. Those who put in a good word give a positive endorsement of an other. Those who eat their words are paying for their verbal transgressions. To have words with another is to argue and a word to the wise is sufficient. Having the last word puts one in a position of power. These and many other popular sayings about words reveal their prominence and forcefullness in our everyday life.

We previously noted that word use is predominately a talent of the left brain. Particularly as words are woven into the structure of our language they lend themselves to the expression of rational, linear thinking processes. In this function, they lead us farther and farther away from our not so rational, emotive responses to things.

At worst, words can be used to deliberately deceive or distort. They can serve our manipulative, exploitative aims quite well.

When Alice of Wonderland fame met Humpty Dumpty she encountered in him the personification of word misuse and abuse. When she challenged his definition of "glory" as meaning a nice knockdown argument, he retorted, "When I use a word, it means just what I choose it to mean—neither more nor less." Like Humpty, we are all inclined to take similar license with words.

Words at their very roots, however, are not easily manipulated, nor are they so far removed from feelings. Etymology, the study of the derivation of words, can lead us back to the sometimes mysterious, sometimes astounding origin of words where the lexical and enactive modes seem to blend.

At that point, words transcend their place in language. They open to us new vistas of imagery, the imagery that preceded the uttered sound and written symbol. That image remains embedded in every word we speak.

At root level, words become intense stimuli for imagery which may reveal to the imagist the hidden nuances and emotive source of the word itself. If it is a favored and/or often used component of the imagist's vocabulary, it may then have to be employed with a new awareness that has an impact on the personality and world view of the user. That a single word can wield such influence lends further credence to the long established belief that there is an incredible power in words .

The clinical procedure upon which we are concentrating involves the private eye in an investigation of a word or words having special significance, be it positive or negative, to the ego. Sometimes it is difficult for the client to identify such words because they are used spontaneously with a high degree of comfort and a low degree of awareness. However, if those who are working alone on this exercise are willing to pay close attention to the their speech patterns it is very likely that several significant words will be turned up.

The procedure is easier if you are working with a therapist or trusted other. Careful listening should enable your helper to identify some words or phrases which you use repetitively or with extraordinary emotional overlay.

Once such a word has been identified by either client or therapist, the mission is to encounter it fully in terms of the client's conscious perception of it in its present form and at its origin. The steps to be taken are as follows:

1. The client is relaxed.

2. It is suggested that the client concentrate on the designated word intently and, then, let it go while allowing any image which arises to become the focus of attention.

3. The client is encouraged to work with the image by allowing feelings about it to surface, by taking some kind of action in regard to it or by entering into dialogue with it in the manner described in previous chapters.

4. If the imagery work seems meaningful and productive, in follow-up suggest that the client investigate the etymology of the word/stimulus. She can be directed to the many dictionaries and books on word origins available at any library.

5. When the patient returns with information on the word, guide her on an imagery journey that incorporates the new data which has been discovered.

Since I am no expert on etymology, I am usually as surprised as the patient by what is turned up. The really uncanny thing is that, frequently, the patient's original imagery has incorporated some essence of the word's root, a phenomenon which has helped to convince me of the validity of Jung's synchronicity and the collective unconscious.

Through the years, I've gathered some remarkable examples in my case files which have relevance here.

The Case of the Thing in the Woods

Leon was a young man just out of college who was working in his father's insurance firm. Always tense and nervous, he had his first severe anxiety attack after smoking pot at a fraternity party during his sophomore year. His attacks became more frequent and severe until he was put on anti-anxiety medicine. He came to see me because he wanted to get to the bottom of his problem and get off of the medicine.

Leon used the word "panic" repetitively. He was not using it in accordance with the clinical definition. He would say, "I panicked," over this, that or the other thing. He made statements like, "I can hear the panic in my voice when I start to get up-tight." He described an amusing buddy as "a panic."

I called his attention to his frequent use of the word and said, in view of his illness, it was understandably an important word to him. I invited him to use it as a stimulus for imagery.

After concentrating on the word, Leon developed an image of himself lost in the woods at night. He had the distinct sensation of being stalked by some kind of animal. He became tremulous and sweating as he heard it thrashing about in the brush. He thought it might be something like a bear or a wildcat but he knew, somehow, that it had the intelligence of a man. Whatever it was, it remained concealed.

In our follow-up, I suggested that an investigation of the word's origin might help in some way to clarify its prominence in his vocabulary. Leon was intrigued and returned the following week with surprising news.

He had learned that "panic" was derived from the Greek word PANIKOS, meaning "of Pan." He vaguely recollected that Pan was a creature with the lower body of a goat and the upper body of a man.

Further mythological research revealed that Pan was the guardian of the forest and not above playing pranks on travelers who found themselves in the woods at night. He liked to terrify them by pretending to be a goblin.

On the positive side, Pan was revealed to be a creative deity whose essence pervaded all things in nature, including the pastures, flocks and herds. Leon laughed reassuredly as he announced that he was certain his pursuer in the woods had been Pan at play.

All of this had the effect of enabling Leon to return in imagery to the forest where he sought, found and befriended Pan. Pan became his guide, teaching him of the peace and oneness with the entirety of Nature which could be so richly experienced in the forest. This turned out to be an important adjunct to Leon's psychotherapy.

The Case of the Clever Dunce

I recall one occasion on which my knowing a word origin may have immediately helped a patient reframe an ego damaging incident. It involved twelve year old Sammy who was a bright (I.Q. 110) but fractious youngster from an emotionally deprived home environment. He was a difficult but articulate and knowledge seeking child.

Sammy was having problems with his middle school teachers, a fact reflected in his grades. The classroom problem was that he digested facts and concepts more quickly than most of his classmates. Wanting to discuss the material being taught, he would ask many questions and seek to gather more details than the teacher or other children wanted to pursue. Thwarted in his efforts, he became sulky, restless, and inclined to clown around for attention. His current teachers believed he was doing all of this to cover up a lack of comprehension.

When Sam appeared in my office, he immediately impressed me as being unusually bright yet, whenI asked him to draw a picture of himself, he depicted himself seated on at his desk, wearing a dunce's cap as the teacher pointed her ruler at him and the other children laughed. I inquired into what the drawing meant.

"My English teacher says I'm a dunce," he said. "She showed the class a dunce hat like kids used to have to wear when they didn't get their lessons. Some of the kids said, 'Give it to Sam,' and she laughed. So, I guess she thinks I'm a dunce."

"Perhaps you are," I said, "but not in the way your classmates and teacher are suggesting. You and they may not know it, but that word comes from the name of man who lived many centuries ago. His name was John Duns Scotus and he taught at the most famous universities in England and in France because he was a brilliant philosopher."

Sammy was immediately interested. "How did he get to be a dunce?"

"The trouble is," I continued, "after he died, his followers became sort of pig-headed in their opposition to many of the changes that were going on at the time and lots of people didn't like them. They started calling them 'Duns' men' and that got to be 'dunces.'

"Remember, though, these guys weren't dumb. They just had unpopular opinions. I guess you could say they just didn't go along with what everyone else said. They had a different viewpoint.

"Anyway, if your teacher is trying to tell you you are dumb, it's just not so. In fact, by calling you a dunce, she's saying it's not so. The father of the dunces was a very smart professor and his followers were smart, too, but maybe a bit too outspoken."

Shortly after that meeting, Sammy's family moved from the area so I have no way of knowing if the new image of Duns Scotus replaced his image of himself in a pointed hat. I remember that, after telling the boy that story, he said to me, "I'm a lot smarter than they give me credit for."

The Case of the Different Drum

I had no idea where it would lead when I sent Eric on a word hunt. He was in his thirties, shy and soft spoken with a non-existent social life. He liked nature photography and spent his week-ends alone in search of plants and wildlife.

Eric maintained that his lifestyle was very much to his liking but I suspected a masked depression. His parents, worried about him, had encouraged him to seek therapy.

"They just don't understand me," he said. " A lot of people don't. I happen to march to the beat of a different drum."

That turned out to be a recurrent phrase from Eric. When confronted with his atypical attitudes he would say he marched to a different drum.

When this patient used "drum" as a stimulus, he imaged a magnificent parade drum, booming majestically as he marched in a one man review while spectators cheered him on.

In follow-up, he identified his fantasy as, perhaps, a bit grandiose, but said he liked it. He agreed to track down the origin of "drum."

I don't believe that he ever got to the root of the word itself because, in his investigations, he discovered that, in the East Indian country of Madras, there was a class of people who inherited the task of beating the drum, which was called a PARAI.

This same class traditionally worked as house servants for Europeans living in that country. The employers regarded the drum beaters or PARIAHS as the dregs of society lending the meaning "social outcast" to the word, PARIAH.

This information had a powerful effect on Eric who immediately identified with the PARIAHS. He was overtly depressed at his next session as he described what he had uncovered.

"Who am I kidding?" he asked. "I'm not marching to a different drum—I'm not even marching. I'm one of them. Nobody wants to be associated with me. The truth is, I feel inferior to just about everybody - and...I'm very, very lonely."

Eric's search for his different drum had resulted in a major break in his defensive wall. He was now ready to image the pariah within him, beginning a series of productive sessions which culminated in the alleviation of his depression.

The Case of the Second Place Equestrian

More often than not, word imagery leads to insights far less dramatic than Eric's. When this is so, the client still may be enriched by it.

Rita was approaching thirty when she came to therapy. Her blond hair and fair skin to which she applied no make-up contributed to a washed out appearance and her soft way of speaking did not command attention. Predictably, she described herself as passive and anxiety riddled.

She worked as a librarian and was still living with her parents. Her social life was nil.

The single pursuit in which Rita felt confident was horseback riding. She had been given her first horse by her father when she was eleven and had ridden in amateur competitions throughout her teens.

By her late teens, Rita was an accomplished equestrian, but, incredibly, she never won first place at any of the horse shows in which she competed. Second was the best she ever did. It seems uncanny that she always managed to make some mistake significant enough to prevent her from getting a trophy but such is the power of unconscious programming.

Sometimes the phrase, "You never got a trophy," resounded obsessively in her mind. When she imaged a trophy, it was in the context of having won a competition but when she had it in hand it turned out to be small and cheap looking and she threw it into a drawer. Following that imagery, she sought the origin of the word "trophy."

Rita's etymological journey took her back to the Greek word TROPE, signifying the turning point in a battle. A derivative of TROPE was the word TROPAION, which described a monument erected on a battlefield at the exact spot where the enemy was put to flight. The monument was usually made up of discarded arms flung aside by the fleeing enemy. So "trophy," she discovered harkens back to a symbol of victory in war.

"What I learned," said the client, "is that, at a deeper level, the trophy for horsemanship is not what's really important to me. Once, just once, I want to win one of life's big battles. I want to be a real success at something. I want to have friends. I want to stop being so god-awfully afraid of everything."

In the imagery that followed, Rita began giving herself imaged trophies for each little victory she achieved in combatting her anxiety and withdrawal. On a more concrete level she began constructing her own tropaion.

She saved mementos of her positive actions: ticket stubs from the theater, the resume and letter of introduction she used to secure a better job, souvenirs from places to which she traveled, cards from people she sought as friends. These were the hard earned, meaningful trophies she really wanted, each one designating a turning back of the enemy: fear.

The Case of the Saintly Whore

Word imagery can sometimes have an astounding effect on therapeutic work. A patient of a few years ago named Priscilla provides a case in point. She came to me for help at age twenty-two, tall, blond and voluptuous—one of the most beautiful women I have ever seen.

She was dressed seductively, wore a bit too much make-up and was overladen with jewelry. Her short hemline showed off her shapely legs to good advantage as she sat down and crossed them. She started out the interview provocatively.

"You're not going to believe this," she said, "but I'm an honest-to-goodness virgin."

"Why do you think I won't believe you?" I asked.

"Nobody does, especially in my family," she replied. "They think I'm the biggest little whore in town."

As Priscilla told her story, her countenance and manner became less that of the sultry seductress and more that of a vulnerable little girl. She related that her entire childhood had been spent in the shadow of her older sister, Kate, whom she described as a natural beauty with superior intelligence.

Kate was everthing her parents wanted and admired in an offspring. She was popular with both peers and adults, a born leader and a dutiful daughter. Recently, Kate had become the mother of an apple dumpling baby girl, the first grandchild.

While her sister was openly adored, Priscilla was regarded as the problem child. Her mother described her as being fractious and oppositional, even in infancy. Mother was especially upset by the girl's disregard for the social graces and father expressed great disappointment over her "average" academic performance. They compared her with her sister frequently and unfavorably.

Throughout her early life, the client felt she had no resources for competing with her sibling. She tried very hard to be not like her but, according to her parents' values, that meant being bad and disagreeable.

Things began to change when Priscilla reached an early and dramatic puberty. Seemingly overnight, she blossomed magnificently.

It soon became apparent to her that she now had a means of getting attention, particularly from males, which surpassed her wildest dreams. She began to capitalize on her budding sexuality in every way she could think of. She dressed tauntingly and flirted shamelessly.

Immediately, she was dubbed "wild" and "boy crazy" by her parents who tightened up their restrictions even in regard to her attending school functions. When the girl did get away from home, she often managed to have furtive petting sessions. She found the sexual sensations moderately interesting but what really thrilled her was the awareness of someone avidly desiring her.

Priscilla was probably well on her way to having intercourse when a crisis changed her direction. Ironically, the crisis centered on Kate.

My client was fifteen and Kate seventeen at the time. In a state of anxiety, the older girl confided to Priscilla that she and her steady boyfriend of the past year had been having sex relations and that she feared she might be pregnant.

Despite a promise that she would not do so, Priscilla lost no time in revealing Kate's plight to their mother. She hoped that, at last, the favorite daughter might be toppled from her pedestal.

The parental response was quite the opposite. Mom and dad confronted Kate with maximum concern and emotional support. They sympathized with her for the "ordeal" she had been going through and, when it was verified that she was not pregnant, they gave her a vote of confidence, saying she had learned a valuable lesson which they knew would not be repeated.

In spite of the outcome, Priscilla concluded that Kate had shown her feet of clay and that, finally, there was a way she could best her. She made a decision to remain a virgin until she married.

Nevertheless, the girl continued to flaunt her physical charms and earned herself among the males in her peer group the reputation of being a tease. Despite this, she stuck to her guns even when doing so involved considerable effort as in a couple of "close call" wrestling matches.

After the Kate crisis, the parents watched Priscilla even more closely. They issued warnings that she was riding for a fall. A few times, her mother openly accused her of "fooling around" with this or that boy.

When Priscilla acted indignant and hurt, mother took a "oh, come off it" attitude. When she avowed being a virgin she was told sarcastically by her mother that she was the kind of virgin who should be on the pill.

In the midst of much rancor, Priscilla moved out of her parents' home immediately after her high school graduation. She and a girl friend shared a small apartment and she went to work as a waitress at a popular nightclub. She was a favorite of the patrons and with generous tips made a good living. She worked long hours and had few dates. She kept her relationships with males superficial.

Keeping it a secret from her parents and almost everyone else, Priscilla continued to practice the Roman Catholic Religion in which she had been raised. She was a faithful communicant and very thoughtful about spiritual matters.

Priscilla came to therapy because she was unhappy about her estrangement from her parents, her lifestyle and her self image. She wanted to make changes but didn't know where to begin. She wanted to reach out to her family.

She also wanted to drop her seductive facade but feared she would get no more attention from any quarter if she did. She wished she could let people know of her sensitive, compassionate and spiritual side but feared it would inspire ridicule.

In our early explorations, Priscilla recalled an incident that transpired between her and her mother when she was in her senior year. It exemplified their basic misunderstanding and was for the young woman an unhealed psychological wound.

It occured when Priscilla had been invited to an elegant party at the home of a schoolmate whose parents were socially prominent and much respected by her own parents. Such contacts were of special importance to her mother who emphasized the value of making good impressions.

The teenager was eager to make her mother proud by impressing everyone at the party. She set about doing so in the only way she knew.

In her room, she spent hours applying a heavy coat of newly purchased, expensive cosmetics. Then she put on a clingy party dress and several of her best loved pieces of costume jewelry. Thinking she had achieved a uniquely exotic image, she made her way to the living room to await the arrival of her date.

When she entered the room her mom and dad were watching television. Her father glanced up and quickly returned his attention to the screen, shaking his head slightly.

The mother's gaze became riveted on her daughter. She gave a little gasp and rose from her chair to face the child.

For a moment, Priscilla thought she was going to be given a compliment, perhaps a hug. She moved toward her mother, smiling.

"My God," the woman said, groping for words. "You look...you look positively tawdry. I'm so ashamed!"

Tears stung Priscilla's blue eyes. She bit her lip to hold them back. She knew she could not speak without blubbering, so she beat a hasty path to the front porch.

She was thankful to see her pickup car pulling up just as she arrived there. She ran to it and, without inviting her date inside, requested that he get them the hell out of there. The delighted young driver shoved the car in gear and they sped off with a loud screeching of wheels.

The incident was never discussed again but, whenever thereafter the girl got down on herself, the word "tawdry" echoed in her ears. She was not absolutely certain of the definition but she associated it with being cheap and vulgar. It brought forth feelings of deep humiliation and worthlessness.

In view of the word's effect on her and its recurrence, we decided it would be worthwhile for her to image it. The visualization which followed depicted Priscilla naked except for layers of gaudy, glittering jewelry. She was bedecked with earrings, necklaces, bracelets, anklets and a waist band and was lounging on a huge bed with red satin sheets. She realized that she was a prostitute awaiting the arrival of her next trick.

The client was repelled by this image but forced herself to enter into dialogue with it. It identified itself only as "the Whore." It laid claim to being an essential part of Priscilla's self, adding, however, that she should not be deceived by appearances, that there was more to her than meets the eye. After that, she would say no more.

Priscilla and I were both puzzled by the imagery. Feeling a lack of direction about where to go next, I suggested that she investigate the origin of the word "tawdry" to see if it would shed any light. Boy, did it!

The girl came to her next therapy session energized, flushed, excited. "Wait till you hear what I've learned," she bubbled.

She immediately launched into a story about an Anglo-Saxon princess called Aethelthryth who, as a young girl, dedicated her life, body and soul, to God. However, like many princesses, she was expected to enter into a politically advantageous marriage arranged by her father, the king.

Aethelthryth was forced into two such marriages. In both, she successfully fought for and preserved her virginity.

This pure and spiritual woman carried a burden of guilt all of her life based on her youthful addiction to golden chains and necklaces. In maturity she regarded this love of jewelry as sinful vanity. She believed it to be the cause of the throat cancer which finally caused her death in the Seventh Century.

"That's a wonderful story," I said as Priscilla paused to catch her breath, " but what has it to do with your imagery?"

"Just wait," she cautioned. "It's fantastic."

Truly, the rest of the story was fantastic. With the rise of the Normans, Aethelthryth's name was shortened to Audrey as her legend was passed down through the years. Finally, the Church officially canonized her as St. Audrey.

On St. Audrey's Day, October 17, a custom arose of holding fairs to celebrate it. A tradition at these fairs was the selling of lace scarves and golden necklaces which the merchants called St. Audrey's laces. At first, these were quality articles but as time went on they became cheap and showy.

The cry of the hucksters at the fairs was abbreviated from "St. Audrey's lace" to "Sint Audrey lace" to simply "Tawdry lace." Thus, "tawdry" came to stand for any item that was cheap and gaudy.

Entranced by the tale, I asked Priscilla what it meant to her.

"Don't you see?" she queried enthusiastically. "The tawdry woman is a part of me which has been given a bad label because of some of the things I'm addicted to. But, at her roots, Audrey's really a good person and so am I.

"That's why she said I shouldn't be deceived by appearances. I may be a silly girl using sex to get attention but I'm not a whore and she's not either. For God's sake, she's a saint!"

And so it was that Priscilla returned to her imagery and met her Inner Guide, Audrey. Audrey has been the girl's companion and director on a journey of psychospiritual growth which began at that time and has continued to the present. Priscilla perceives Audrey as the representation of her Higher Consciousnes, the symbol of the best that she is and all that she can become.

From the Therapist's Notebook: The Peregrine

While I was imaging with a trusted friend and colleague a hawk suddenly appeared before me. I have great admiration for hawks and was startled and pleased by its abrupt arrival. It assumed a stately pose on the branch of a nearby tree and eyed me up and down.

"We know you," it said in a calm, masculine voice. "You watch us and respect us and we know you."

The bird was alluding to my fascination for watching hawks in the wild from the acreage surrounding our home.

"Thank you for coming into my imagery," I said, really meaning it. "Do you have a name?"

"I am Aeneas," he said matter-of-factly. The name conjured up memories of my high school Latin class but I could not recall exactly what it was that Vergil's hero did.

"And why have you come to me?"

The hawk spread his magnificent wings. "We know that you are going to need help and protection on your journey through the field. We are prepared to assist you.

I wondered which field he was talking about but in my exhiliration forgot to ask. "I welcome your help," I said.

"In order to have it, you must join our Brotherhood as a fledgling."

"What must I do?"

"Come with me."

With that, he swooped and sank his talons painlessly into the flesh of my shoulders. He lifted me high to the top branches of the lofty pine.

I felt unsteady as I balanced on the branch. The ground looked far away.

"Now," said Aeneas, "you must fly with me."

"I am human. I cannot fly," I protested.

"You must rid yourself of such notions," he said. "Spread your wings."

My observing self watched in utter disbelief as my arms slowly began to spread out at my sides. They required no permission from me to do so.

"This is ridiculous," I thought. "It can't be happening."

But it did happen. At full expansion my arms felt like wings and I was aware of the wind beneath them, lifting them. With Aeneas close at my side, I launched and flew!

I have never had a more real sensation of flying. The wind rushed against me and around me.

I was weightless. I soared and I dove and I glided. Aeneas called out what I took to be encouragement in the language of his kind. It was an altogether magical experience.

The duration of the flight was all too brief. I found it deflating to be back on the ground. I felt breathless.

"In time you will be a peregrine. From now on we are Brothers. We shall be constantly near as you you make your way through the field."

My new brother flexed his wings and was gone in an instant. I returned to ordinary consciousness.

The experience had seemed so real that I had to ask my trusted other what had happened. He could tell me only that I had spread out my arms and maintained an ecstatic expression during the flight.

"Are you sure I never left the chair?" I inquired.

"Absolutely," he replied.

A few days later I was reading a magazine article about people making pilgrimages to sites where the Virgin Mary has reputedly appeared. Digressing, the author focused on the origin of the word "pilgrim" and linked it to the Latin word "peregrinus."

The word caught my attention in view of Aeneas' statement that I would eventually become a peregrine which I took to mean a falcon. The interesting thing is that the writer went on to explain that pilgrim, peregrination and similar words were all rooted in two basic Latin words: "per" meaning through and "ager" meaning field.

A sense of the mystical enveloped me as I remembered Aeneas saying so pointedly that the hawks would assist me on my journey "through the field." A pilgrim or peregrine is one who wanders through the fields, far and wide, seeking the Great Mystery.

The gospel writer known as John tells us that the Word is Holy. In the affairs of men, the word is a sacred and binding force. In the minds of men, it is the key to knowledge and enlightenment. In the hearts of men, it is the source of magic and enchantment.

CHAPTER TWELVE

THE OTHER SEX
SELF

Our Innate Duality

The mythologies of the world give accountings of the origin of the universe and mankind. Predominately authored by males, they contain evidence that from earliest times men have been awed by and perhaps envious of the female's ability to become pregnant and give birth. This may well be the basis for the many stories in which the birthing function is usurped by males such as the account of Zeus giving birth to Athena from his head and Dionysus from his thigh.

In the Brihadaranyaka Upanishad of the Hindus, the Great Self is unhappily alone and divides in two, creating man and wife from which all other human beimgs are born. In the Bible, an androgynous Adam grows lonely, leading God to personify his feminine aspect as the woman, Eve, thus providing him with a mate.

In these and many other creation stories, there is a unixsexual source from which the two sexes spring. In their wisdom, the ancients knew that, though physically differentiated, our psychospiritual make-up incorporates both male and female. This was their way of explaining that awarness.

While Nature usually pretty clearly identifies us as male or female at birth, the development of those traits which we label masculine or feminine is determined as much or more by psychosocial variables as by biology. Freud identified an innate bisexuality in all of us which, as influenced by the external environment, potentiates sexual attraction to the same sex and/

or the development of attitudes and behaviors usually associated with the opposite sex.

C.G. Jung shed light on the duality of our sexual nature with his concept of the Anima and Animus as structures which, along with others, make up the human psyche. The Anima is the archetypal image of woman which is present in the unconscious of every male. It evolves from the individual's biological make-up which includes female genes and hormones, his actual experience of woman-kind, and his inherited collective image of man's experience of woman throughout all time. Through recognition and acceptance of this aspect of himself, the male realizes his full vitality, increases receptivity, and enters more deeply into the realm of emotions.

Its counterpart, the Animus is woman's unconscious image of man. It arises from the same sources as the Anima. Through realization of the Animus, woman increases self assertiveness, rationality, responsibility and independence.

If we over-identify with these vestiges of the opposite sex, we may display an appearance and/or behavior inappropriate to our gender. Inescapably, the way we ultimately integrate Animus and Anima will be a determining factor in whether we evolve a hetero, homo or bisexual preference.

If we are to truly know who and what we are, it is essential that we confront our mixed sexual nature for the purpose of understanding and integrating its elements. We may find this disturbing because we live in a culture which is largely homophobic and clings to the fallacious belief that men are men and women are women, denying that there are shades of gray.

I shall never forget the bristling reaction of my client Travis as we discussed the opposites within his personality and the need to get them in balance. He was a plant farmer, a physically large man heavily entrenched in "good old boy" attitudes. I suggested it would be worthwhile for him to develop an image of his feminine side.

"What do you mean, my feminine side?" His voice was more demanding than questioning.

"It's true, Travis," I said cheerily. "All guys have some feminine in their make-up."

He glared at me for several seconds before speaking.

"Aw, shit, man. I'm not buying into this."

"Take it easy," I soothed. "We're not talking about you being gay or anything."

"No?" he looked relieved.

"No. We're talking about the opposites that exist in all of us. Just like the passive and aggressive stuff we discussed before."

"So, let me get this straight. I'm supposed to recognize something feminine in myself?"

"Right and you already have. You remember telling me about the sick calf and how you got so attached to her - bottle feeding her, sitting up nights with her?"

Travis nodded sullenly.

"Well, that's an example of you being very nurturing - mothering. You saved that calf's life and felt good about yourself in that role. You were drawing on that feminine aspect yourself, your Anima, when you did all that."

The farmer's lips relaxed and a slight smile formed.

"I've always been good at taking care of little hurt things," he said proudly. "My mama never had any schooling but she was the best nurse in the whole world."

By the time he completed therapy, Travis was more comfortably integrated with his Anima and, to the delight of his wife and children, seemed to be enjoying speding more time with them around the house. It remains doubtful that he has ever gotten into a discussion of his Anima with his hunting and fishing buddies.

In my clinical practice, I encounter many men like Travis who react with anxiety and resistance to the revelation that they have a feminine component. Right away, they become concerned that I am saying they are latently homosexual which, of course, is not the case. Generally, women are less threatened by the Animus but, for all of us, actively encountering our other sex self tends to be unsettling.

People who believe themselves to be all male or female are, in fact, fragmented. Their personhood lacks authenticity and their persona is apt to burlesque the real meaning of masculinity or femininity.

Similarly out of balance are those who energize the opposite sex within, but portray only the most negative aspects of it. The result may be a tough, demanding and callous woman who attempts to be one of the boys or a yielding, emotional and dependent male incapable of bonding with other males.

A balanced integration of anima and animus brings out the best in people. This was entertainingly confirmed in the 1982 motion picture, *Tootsie* (Columbia), in which Dustin Hoffman portrays an abrasive actor who masquerades as a woman in order to secure a performing job. In the course of carrying out this charade, the Anima of the actor is brought to the surface and he is transformed into a decent and likeable human being.

Imagery provides an effective tool for discovering and working with our male and female components. The case of Lois will illustrate.

The Case of the Bone, the Club and the Disk

Her full name was Lois Pitchford. At age thirty-five she came to me in the throes of breaking up with her boyfriend of two years duration. For the third time in her adult life, she was experiencing the loss of a man she loved and respected. She wanted to figure out what she was doing wrong.

Lois was a prosecutor with the State Attorney's Office. She was known as a tough litigater. She liked to win. It didn't much bother her that the male attorneys at her office called her "Pitchfork" behind her back. She took satisfaction in knowing that many male attornies were afraid to go up against her in court.

Lois was above averagely attractive and made sure she looked her best when she appeared before the bench. She had a "snappy" manner and was much given to sarcasm and wise cracks. She held in utter contempt men whom she perceived as lacking ambition or self esteem.

She turned on sexually to physically large males who didn't waste too much time on foreplay when they made love to her. She responded orgasmically about fifty per cent of the time, but that was not an issue of great importance to her.

In the course of assessing herself, this client concluded that she didn't have a very good understanding of what constitutes masculine and feminine behavior. She had grown up in a close relationship with her father who was also an attorney and physically present in the home only on a limited basis. He justified his absences on the grounds that he intended to be very successful in his field. He eventually became a highly regarded professor of law at Tulane.

When Lois referred to her mother, she used the epithet "Sally Homemaker." She reflected disgust with her mother's dependent lifestyle and "trivial" concerns about her social activites and volunteer work. She blamed her mother for making a sissy of her younger brother who was a declared homosexual. She could see why her father chose not to be around very much.

By the time she reached her teens, Lois was successfully competing with males in athletics and in the classroom. She had several male friends but no close girl friends. None of the males looked upon her as "special." They would socialize with her in groups, but no one sought to date her on a one to one basis.

"Pitchfork" did not have intercourse until she was twenty and in college. She met her first lover who was a graduate student at a campus hangout. They engaged in some impassioned debates over frosted mugs of beer. They both had a gift for words and delighted themselves and each other with their repartee.

He was over six feet tall and quite intellectual. They went steady for about a year before a cute little southern belle type caught his eye. When he terminated the relationship, he told Lois the debating had become boring and that she really had nothing else to offer.

Lois was crushed by his rejection and withdrew from social life until she graduated. She had no difficulty gaining admission to Law School and was an outstanding student.

She developed an interest in a couple of male students during the course of her professional education. They seemed to greatly enjoy contact with her as a colleague but to her secret disappointment showed no romantic inclinations.

She began her career as a public defender, but signed on as a prosecutor after a few years. In that capacity, her legal talents reached fruition.

Her next attempt at intimacy was with a lawyer from the private sector with a community reputation for being a hot-shot. They met as courtroom adversaries and he got his client acquitted in a hard fought case. Impressed by Lois' talents, he invited her out for a "bury the hatchet" dinner and they began seeing each other regularly.

This gentleman, Justin, was a divorcee in his forties, big but out of shape and balding. He had a booming voice and an excessively aggressive manner. Lois thought he was wonderful.

After about a year, what started out as an exciting, stimulating relationship began to grow painful for my client. Justin, who had proved to be a heavy drinker, became increasingly unwilling to let her have the last word on any issue. He would vehemently argue any point of disagreement, determined to "win."

Lois, while ordinarily taking delight in controversey, was hurt and dismayed by the lengths to which Justin would go, especially the leveling of deeply personal criticisms of her. She attempted to communicate to him that many of her verbal challenges were a form of intellectual play and that he didn't have to go for the jugular. It made no difference. His hostility toward her grew increasingly noxious.

On a couple of occasions "Pitchfork" broke down emotionally during an epsiode of conflict and Justin reacted with total disgust. He said if there was one thing he couldn't stand it was a "whimpering cunt."

Within six months, he was seeing other women. When Lois protested, he suggested they break up. She begged him to work with her on the relationship, but he refused. His parting words were, "See you in court."

Just prior to consulting me, Lois had been maintaining a relationship with a detective from the police department. They had done some investigative work together and established one of those bantering, you-piss-me-off kinds of relationship which is so popular in the movies. Of course, they were both getting off on their interaction and drawing closer all the time.

Ted, the cop, was less cerebral and more animalistic than his predecessors. In time, he dropped the verbal sparring and sought greater expressions of emotion and sexual feeling from the attractive attorney.

Lois had no idea how to go about meeting those needs though she wanted to please him. She did her best to lure him back into the familiar fun of verbal jousting, but it didn't work.

With a heavy heart, she watched him drift away. For a time she denied it to herself, but she finally faced up to the fact that he was seeing someone else. This time, she ended the relationship and made a commitment to solving her underlying problem, whatever the hell it was.

After gathering these facts, I started our next therapy session by asking Lois to engage in a brief interlude of relaxation. This accomplished, I suggested that she allow an image of her femininity to form on her inner movie screen. I cautioned her not to force it and to accept anything that appeared without question or censorship whether it turned out to be animal, vegetable or mineral. I told her to trust her unconscious to send her a symbol that she could learn from and work with.

It took her only a few moments to report that she was looking down at what appeared to be the floor of her apartment and could see a very tiny piece of bone laying there. She snorted, proclaiming, "This is totally ridiculous."

A piece of bone! I was inclined to agree with her about the inanity of it, but was also filled with curiosity about its meaning.

"What will you do with that piece of bone?" I asked.

"I guess...I guess I'll pick it up and examine it and see if I can figure out where the hell it came from."

"O.K. Do that and tell me what happens."

"Well (Pause), It's barely visible. It's kind of triangular.(Longer Pause) I know! It's that little bone in the ear, the one shaped like a stirrup."

"Yes," I affirmed. "It's called the stapes. What are you inclined to do with it?

"I don't know. I wonder where it came from."

"It's yours," I said reflectively.

"Why would I lose that, of all things?"

"If you like, you can ask the little bone why it's come to you. Then, be patient and wait for an answer."

"O.K." Lois fell silent for the better part of a minute. During that time, her facial expression grew serious, her brow furrowed.

"The stirrup says I can't hear without it. I've lost it because there is something I don't want to hear."

"See if you can find out what that is," I suggested.

"I already did. It's myself. The bone says if I really listened to myself I wouldn't like what I hear. I've got to figure out a way to put it back in my ear."

"Why don't you put the little bone some place that's safe so you can come back and work with it some more later?"

"O.K. I'm putting it in my change purse."

"Have you got it there?"

"Yes."

"Good. Now, will you allow an image of your masculine self to appear?"

"O.K." Soon she was caught up in laughter.

"What are you in touch with?" I asked.

"Oh, no. This is too disgustingly Freudian. I don't even want to tell you."

"It's important that you don't censor," I reminded her.

"I feel stupid. It's a big wooden club - the kind the stereotypical caveman carries around - obviously a phallic symbol."

"Stay away from interpretations for now. Thank the club for appearing."

"Thanks for appearing, you big hard thing," she said sarcastically.

"What are you prepared to do with it?" I inquired.

Lois sucked her lower lip between her teeth and was thoughtful for a few seconds. "It's not good for much except bashing things. I guess I'll pick it up."

I remained briefly silent while she worked with her image.

"You know," she said, " this mother's really heavy. It's so unwieldy I couldn't land a well aimed blow with it. At best, I can just swing it around."

"What happens when you do that?"

"Well, anybody around will have to stand back. Somebody really strong could take it away from me, but most people are going to be intimidated by it."

"Will you put your club somewhere safe so that we can come back to it and work with it some more?"

"Sure. It belongs in a cave and there just happens to be one here. I'll stick it right inside the entrance."

When this was accomplished, I told her I would like her to deal with one more image. I asked her to get in touch with a symbol of her male and female parts united.

This image took longer in arriving than the others. When it did, Lois seemed again perplexed.

"It's a record," she said, "a phonograph record. It's one of those large 33 1/3 plastic records."

"What will you do with it?"

She shrugged. "Play it, I guess."

"Can you find a phonograph?"

"Yes."

I waited while she put the record on and listened to it briefly.

"Can you hear the music?"

"Yes. It's rock."

"Is that your kind of music?"

"I hate it. It all sounds dissonant to me and its always played too loud. I'm cutting it off." She looked annoyed.

"Please put the record somewhere safe," I requested.

Initially, she indicated that she was placing it beneath the cushion of the chair on which she was seated. I cautioned that someone might sit on it and break it. She chuckled at that possibility, recognizing her unconscious wish to get rid of it.

Finally, she placed the record in a drawer with her lingerie. We concluded the imagery exercise.

At the time, Lois and I were unaware of the rich store of therapeutic meaning enfolded in those images. They became the central focus of our work for several sessions.

We took the position that all of the images were messages from her unconscious containing information which would help her to both identify and solve problems related to her masculine/feminine balance. In subsequent work, she revisualized them and got into extensive dialogue with them.

She recognized from the beginning that the little stapes bone had appeared to tell her she was avoiding listening to herself. As she made a conscious effort to note her verbalizations, she was appalled by the harsh voice tones and biting comments that came out of her at times. She identified her verbal habits as unattractive and decidedly not feminine.

Her interaction with the ear bone did not stop there. She sought to unravel its total connection with her femininity. After all, it was sent as a representation of her feminine aspect.

As she was made aware that the stapes is the smallest bone in the body, she concluded that it was communicating the shrunken state of her femininity and its relegation to a difficult to access portion of her being. The fact that it was reachable through a bodily orifice took on special meaning, too.

The stapes, being a bone located in the head, revealed to Lois that she was attempting to deal with her femininity in her head, that is, intellectually. The lesson it imparted was that femininity, is an aspect of her total being and should permeate her entire body. The focal point should be her vaginal orifice, not a place in her head.

Even though the tiny stirrup represented the client's minimization of her femininity it was, among all of her images connected with masculine/feminine, the only one composed of living matter. This, said the stapes, should reassure her that her feminine aspect is still alive and, with nurturance, can grow.

After covering these points, Lois decided to place the bone inside her ear. As she imaged doing so, a visualization of her entire skeleton appeared. She interpreted that to mean that reclaiming her feminine aspect would make the superstructure of her being complete and strong. Over a period of time, she would "flesh it out."

The young woman's Freudian club was no less informative. As a representation of her masculine side, it's cumbersomeness pointed out her heavy handed application of masculine traits. She became more clear regarding her problem with males.

She could see that her symbolic wielding of that primitive masculine weapon offended or intimidated most males and many females. Those men that were not so affected probably saw in her a challenge to be taken up or an opportunity for comraderie with a fellow warrior. The club taught that most men probably did not see her as a female object of love or eroticism. It pointed out that Lois did not see herself in this light either.

The primitive nature of the "cave man's club" (Note the double entendre referring to the weapon and to membership in a male society.) led her to identify it as an archaic and irrelevant defensive tool. She decided to leave it in the cave and seek a more appropriate vehicle for expressing her masculine side.

The little stirrup bone had reminded her that she used to enjoy horseback riding and led her to an image of trotting along on a white Arabian stallion. She found a riding crop in her hand and noted that it felt much better than the oversize club.

This image suggested to her that she could "ride" her masculine self, moving forward aggressively but gracefully, inciting admiration more than fear. She could also "dismount" from it and exercise her femininity more freely and fully.

The record turned out to be a metaphor for the "dissonance" in the marriage between Lois' masculine and feminine aspects. Its plasticity symbolized the phoniness with which she displayed both spheres. She, too, was loud and failing to project her true self in concert.

In dialogue, as the client fretted over what to do about what was already indelibly recorded, the record pointed out to her that it had a flip side. When she played it, she got Dvorak. Classical music was her favorite.

The lesson of her imagery was that she needed to turn over. Her task was to construct more feminine attitudes and behaviors on the solid foundation of her femaleness and to give up her hopeless goal of being one of the boys. With effort, she gradually brought into balance her Animus and energized her feminine traits.

At the point of termination, for the first time in her life Lois had a female friend. She expressed confidence that in time she would have the kind of relationship with the opposite sex she had always desired.

At our final session, Lois shed a few tears. It was the first time I had seen her cry.

"In keeping with the turn over to my flip side," she said, "I want you to know this imagery stuff really touched me. I didn't mention it at the time because I thought it was too corny—too feminine, I suppose—but there was one moment which really made my heart soar.

"It was when I first turned that rock record over and heard the other side. I hadn't thought about that piece of music in years, but there it was. It was 'Dvorak's Ninth Symphony.' It's known as the 'New World Symphony.' I knew from that moment I was about to discover a New World of my own."

"Pitchfork's" masculine/feminine aspects were far from being fully integrated when she left treatment, but she and I knew that she had the basic tools for accomplishing it. I have confidence that she has continued to use imagery techniques on her own and that, if she gets stuck somewhere along the way, she will be back to see me.

Imaging Your Three Sexes

Those of you who wish to engage in this kind of imagery should be prepared to follow through over several sessions if your goal is to further integration. Many people receive images which are not so highly symbolized as the ones encountered by Lois, but they are still worthy of further attention.

For example, one woman imaged her feminine aspect as herself in a frilly little dress. This seemed very uninstructive to her until she went back and dialogued with the image. Only then did she discover that the self in the frilly dress was herself at puberty and that her experience of being feminine depended entirely on seeing herself as an undeveloped woman.

A recently divorced male client imaged his masculinity as a sword, a symbol which he regarded as too commonplace to be worthy of attention. He placed it in a sheath at the end of his first encounter with it and found, upon return, that he could not withdraw it. This led to an awareness of an obsessive fear regarding AIDS and other venereal diseases which he did not know he had.

The image is the lesson. The lesson may reinforce something already known or it may be a profound revelation..

If you are working alone, the following procedure will allow you to get maximum benefit from this exercise. If you are a therapist or helper simply present the following steps as instructions:

> 1. Spend a short time relaxing by means of any relaxation procedure familiar to you.
>
> 2. Beginning with your own gender, allow an image of your masculine or feminine aspect to appear. Wait for it patiently and accept whatever comes without censorship.
>
> > a. Treat the image with respect and decide how you wish to interact with it, e.g., talk to it, touch it, etc.
> > b. Carry out the action and observe what takes place without interpreting.
> > c. Leave the image in some safe place so that you can return to it later.
>
> 3. Allow an image of your opposite aspect to appear and proceed through steps a, b and c with it.
>
> 4. Allow an image of your masculine and feminine aspect combined to appear and proceed through steps a, b and c again.
>
> 5. Evaluate the imagery cognitively in order to identify problem areas and unanswered questions. Return to the images as many times as necessary to work through the problems and answer the questions. Let the images themselves assist you. For example, ask your masculine image what you need to do in order to put it in better balance with your feminine side.

From the Therapist's Notebook: Who Was That Woman?

The newest image in my life is the Oriental Woman. I made a valiant effort to ignore her though I did not realize I was doing so.

The effort was to no avail. She would not and will not let me be.

She first appeared in a night dream. She and I were the parents of a family troupe of entertainers who traveled about performing ethnic dances.

I alone was aware of a great deceit I was practicing. I alone knew that I was not her real spouse.

After one of our performances I kissed her on the cheek, told her the truth and apologized for misleading her. I told her she deserved better and departed from her.

A conscious review of the dream revealed to me that I felt extremely unready to interact with this the feminine aspect of my own personality. She had just made herself manifest and I had opted for an immediate divorce.

She next appeared as I sought to visualize my Inner Child. She came to me as a six year old and took me to a restaurant where she and other oriental children danced for the entertainment of the patrons.

I told myself this was insignificant imagery and did no further work with it but my choice to ignore my mysterious female could not be sustained. She kept appearing in various guises.

The next time she visited me she was decidedly Japanese. She was a pop singer with an all-girl rock group. She sang a sexy love song to another member of the group. Not only was she a woman, she was a woman who loved other women.

This image frightened me. I was being confronted with my Anima as a warm. sensuous, mysterious woman. She was artist, singer, dancer—giver and receiver of physical delights. She was wisdom, schooled in the unfamiliar ways of the East. To embrace her would be to acknowledge all of this as part of me.

In imagery I invited her to my special place, the tree beside the little pond on our ranch. She came to me in her youth with flowing black tresses and a radiant beautiful face Her voluptuous form was sheathed in a sari. I held out my arms as she moved slowly toward me.

I experienced a profound sense of completeness as we hugged. "Who are you?" I whispered.

"Delta," she replied softly.

"Shall we be traveling together from now on?" I queried.

"Yes," she said, "I have much to teach you that is new."

CHAPTER THIRTEEN

LABYRINTHS AND CAVERNS FOR TWO

There are various means by which one individual may include another on an imagery journey. To do so is like admitting someone to a usually locked closet where one's most personal possessions are stored.

Most of us feel it is extremely self revealing just to verbalize about inner experience. It is even riskier to bring someone else along to explore our imagination's landscape and its inhabitants firsthand. When both parties are completely open to the experience it is an act of intense intimacy.

After all, the labyrinths and caverns of the mind are the most secret recesses of the Self. There are dark corners which we ourselves are reluctant to investigate much less allow another person to look into them. We have a sense of something evil, totally unacceptable, dwelling there alongside the good in us. Our basic insanity, the legacy from the pre-rational epoch of human evolution, prowls about there.

Civilization has taught us that the mind-place is much to be feared. Our uncensored thoughts and feelings don't obey society's rules about what is o.k. At some level of our being we are all deviant. We fear knowing that and having it known by others. Through our efforts to avoid our dark corners, we ignore or suppress a lot of our inner experience and, thereby, lose touch with much of the untamed beauty and eternal wisdom that lies within the territory.

When the doors of the caverns are opened to another, the perspective changes. There is recognition on both sides that we have entered a chamber from which the humanity of ourselves and all others has sprung. We encounter the collective experience of our species and we are close to our source.

People, alone or with others, who initially visit these deep, dark recesses with apprehension, tend to revere them as a sacred place once their fear has subsided Most want to go back again and again.

Therapuetic assistance toward overcoming the fear of exploration begins with helping the client to recognize the richness of what he is encountering. Through the act of imaging he is quickly able to come face to face with parts of himself that he has previously avoided. Ultimately, this will lead him to an altered concept of himself. He is given the opportunity to expand the boundaries of his being.

Imagery, more than any other method of self exploration confirms that personality is an example of multiplicity in unity— in our oneness we have many subselves. This multiplicity is not pathological. It is the norm rather than the exception.

In confronting our multiplicity, we may find aspects of ourselves that we regard as less than appealing or downright unacceptable. In the aggregate, these rejected fragments of our being form our Shadow, the dark, unrecognized aspect of our personalities. By confronting and integrating our Shadow, we attain wholeness and authenticity.

Keep in mind that our multiplicity is not all on the dark side. There is within each of us a higher consciousness and even a spark of the divine which imagery frequently calls forth.

Through both Shadow and Higher Consciousness the imaging client learns that there is more to her makeup than previously realized. The lesson is complete when she recognizes the acceptability of various parts of her self being in opposition. Prior to that awareness, the person may have expended vast amounts of energy and done herself emotional damage by trying to eradicate contradictions and ambivalences which are funda-mental to human nature.

It is refreshingly unstressing to come to terms with the fact that it is part of our human nature to be, among other things, both passive and aggressive, dependent and independent, smart and stupid, loving and hateful. These contradictions pose no difficulty once we accept them as normal and strive to keep them in balance in our lives.

While the client confronts this truth, the therapist acts as guide, giving reassurance: "Yes, that's how you are; that's how I am, too. So are we all." In time, the client discovers and relies on his own Inner Guide rather than the therapist to give encouragement. How to make contact with the Inner Guide is the subject of Chapter Fourteen.

Group Imagery Technique

Group imagery allows us to share our multiplicity with others in a very direct way. It can be a profoundly moving experience for all of the participants.

I introduce some clients into a therapy group in which imagery is used without any prior preparation. Some enter a group after having had some imagery experience during one- to-one therapy. The prior experience is by no means a prerequisite because group members tend to be strongly supportive of each other and many times are able to allay a newcomers anxiety about imaging more effectively than the therapist alone. I have successfully employed imagery techniques in outpatient therapy groups as well as with couples and family groups.

The simplest approach to using imagery in a group is to have the imaging client describe and interact with his images just as in the one-to-one setting. Those present hear and observe what is going on but do not communicate with the client until the follow-up at which time they can ask questions and give input regarding what they observed, their reactions, etc.

It is particularly rare to find couples and families who have ever shared imagery material in spite of, or perhaps because of, its profound emotional impact on family members. For example, mutual observation of imaging the Child Within can be a moving and enlightening experience for a husband and wife or between parent and child, especially as youngsters get their first validated glimpse of the Child within their mom and dad.

It should be noted that I do not get around to using imagery techniques in marriage and family therapy as much as I would like. This is because my point of intervention is so often during a period of crisis in which conflict resolution must take precedence over everything else.

Equally as limiting is the fact that there are many married couples who cannot or will not tolerate the level of intimacy to which image sharing leads. They are too hurt, angry and/or disappointed to pay attention to or respect each other's inner world.

The mere reporting of imagery promotes intimacy but with variations the intimacy level can be intensified. One variation is to have the imaging person take someone from the group along on her journey and to report out loud what is happening to each of them as the imagery progresses.

This technique invites observation and interpretation of how the two of them relate while on the imaged sojourn, what traits and characteristics of the other are stressed, what feeling states emerge and how the two of them are perceived to interact with the various objects, creatures and persons encountered along the way. Discussion of the imagery is reserved for the follow-up session.

The most intense variation is to have two persons agree to image a journey simultaneously. In this case, they will take joint responsibility for structuring the fantasy and for everything that is done and said along the way. They share the reporting of this to the therapist and others in the group.

Many times I have been amazed by the amount of congru-ence achieved by imagers in tandem. They really seem to be exploring the same landscape. Along the way, they may introduce each other to some of their subselves, solve a problem together, or investigate new horizons.

Obviously, this is not an experience anyone will be doing alone. The steps to be taken in carrying out the exercise in a therapeutic setting are as follows. Non-therapist helpers can make necessary modifications.

1. The client is relaxed.
2. The imagery is introduced in one of several ways.

   a. The client is invited to get in touch with an image of some significant other and to see what evolves.
   b. The client is given guided imagery involving the other which is structured to have rel-evance to the relationship which the client has with the other.
   c. The client and the other are invited to simultaneously create some imagery and to verbally interact as their shared imagery unfolds.

3. The usual follow up ensues but includes the other person as an active participant interjecting her thoughts and feelings about the imagery experience along with the client.

These exercises can be put into motion with much or little structure from the therapist. A non-specific instruction such as, "Get a clear image of so-and-so being with you and see what happens from that point," can be used. Conversely, the instruction can be very specific as in "You and so-and-so are on a space ship which is now landing on an unexplored planet. What happens as you emerge onto this new world?"

The technique is particularly helpful when clients who are in serious conflict are teamed up. Defensive barriers between individuals tend to be broken down by the imagery.

If one person is aggressive and the other passive, the instruction might be for the aggressive one to introduce to the other his scared little kid and for the passive one to introduce his King Kong. There are many ways to work. At this point, some examples should prove helpful.

The Case of the Closet Clown

Tony was a depressed, recently divorced, thirty-seven year old personnel manager for a large department store. When he joined the therapy group his sad, passive manner elicited a lot of supportive behaviors from the more "rescuing" members.

This was not the case with Stella, however. She was an attractive, fast talking, aggressive legal secretary who was having difficulty getting along with others. She seemed to take an instant dislike to Tony and in his first session accused him of being a self pitying cry baby. For the next couple of sessions their interaction consisted of throwing verbal barbs at each other.

Soon, Tony was discussing his need to be loved by everyone. When asked how well the group experience was meeting that need, he replied, "Fine, except for Stella."

I commented that their mutual hostility was apparent and asked if he would like to take a risk which might help them to get on another plane. Tony allowed that he didn't think anything would work but that he was willing to do what he could.

I then invited him to take Stella with him on an imaged journey. He said the thought made him anxious but asked how to proceed.

I instructed him in relaxation until his outward tension abated somewhat. He had worked with imagery before so I did not deem it necessary to provide much structure. I asked him to visualize himself and Stella, giving us a verbal description of both images, and, then, allowing some interaction to unfold.

Tony saw himself casually dressed, feeling comfortable in his condo. Responding to the doorbell, he discovered Stella, elegantly attired, looking beautiful. While entertaining this image of her, he acknowledged to the group that he was for the first time allowing himself to notice her good looks.

He gave her a smile and friendly greeting, but she angrily pushed her way inside and said, "All right, where is it?"

"Where is what?" he asked, bewildered.

Impatiently, Stella began to look through the apartment. "What I want," she said. "You know what I want."

"No, I don't," protested Tony. He expressed growing fear that she would destroy something in her search.

After a few moments of prying into this and that, the woman opened a closet door to reveal a jester clad in fool's garb, complete with cap and bells. He leapt forth as if to take a bow and fell on his face. Stella laughed gleefully.

The jester rose and went into a soft shoe number, completely capturing the woman's attention. Tony, feeling great annoyance, looked carefully at the fool's half masked face and, to his astonishment, saw his own features.

As the dance ended, the jester was showered with hugs and kisses from his female admirer. With a good-bye wave, he returned to the closet. Stella turned to face Tony, resuming her expression of disapproval.

During the follow-up, it was Stella who spoke first. "You're right about me, Tony. I don't accept you the way you are because your sadness and seriousness scare the hell out of me.

"I know there is a depressed part of me, too. I keep it controlled by staying busy, busy and by keeping things light and superficial. I insist that all my friends put forth their fun side when I'm with them. I want you to do the same.

"I stay angry with you because you threaten me. If I relate to your depression, my armor might crack. I am demanding that you be a clown or stay the hell away from me."

Tony said he thought he had learned a lot from his imagery. "First of all, it reminded me that I do have a fun side which I've been keeping locked up, especially since my divorce. You see, back in high school I used to be sort of theatrical. I had a pretty good singing voice and got lots of recognition for playing Frank Butler in our senior class production of *Annie Get Your Gun*.

"Anyway, since then I've maintained a couple of song and dance routines that I can do on request. I've always thought they were pretty good—other people seemed to enjoy them too.

"My wife, Trish, never saw me perform like that before we were married, so I was real thrilled when, soon after, some friends asked me to do my shtick at a party. On the way home, my wife told me it was corny and personally embarrassing to her. I was crushed.

"That was just the beginning of what seemed like endless criticism. Trish had a need to put me down every chance she got. Anyway, after the party incident, I made a private vow to never sing again and I haven't. I've also become more introverted and depressed.

"The imagery also made me aware that I feel a strong attraction to Stella and I guess I'm afraid to show her my fun side because she'll just see me as a fool. Actually, the imagery says that she wouldn't be put off by a little foolishnes from me."

The group seemed awe struck by all of the new awareness Tony had derived from his imagery. For the first time in their experience of him, he seemed totally genuine.

"The problem is me," he continued. "I'm terrified of some woman hurting me again. Stella spotted it as soon as I came into the group. She knew I was investing all my energy in feeling bad so I could get sympathy and pity. That's a safe, low risk way to get people to care about me."

This bit of work set into motion changes in the principals involved and in their relationship. Several sessions later, Stella took Tony and, thereby, the rest of us to meet her Sad One, as she called her. The similarity between this aspect of her personality and Tony as we had come to know him was remarkable.

On the other hand, Tony had begun to let go of his woeful facade following his imagery exercise. He was asked and consented to do one of his musical routines for the group. Since we had no musical instrument available, our virtuoso did a lip synch to a recorded number from his big hit in high school, Irving Berlin's *Annie Get Your Gun*. He even threw in a few dance steps.

We all agreed it was wonderful in a corny way and he beamed. The number he performed was called "My Defenses Are Down." I don't know how conscious he was of the title's double meaning but it expressed a great truth.

The Case of the Basement Creature

Imagery shared between family members is often extraordinarily rich in symbolism and reveals the basic structure of relationships within the family. The following case is representative.

Shelly was a fourteen year old girl suffering from recurrent, severe abdominal pains for which no organic basis could be found. Her mother responded to the girl's condition with a display of worry and over protectiveness.

All the while Shelly and her mother obsessed over her physical condition, Ted, the man in their life continued to pursue his rather adolescent lifestyle. He liked to drink in excess and to pursue a social life consisting mostly of drinking in the company of other males.

These activities kept him away from home a lot. When he was around, his relationship with Shelly was that of a playmate, constantly kidding, chasing her and applying a bear hug when he caught her. Seldom willing to be serious about anything, he was constantly making silly remarks to get a laugh from her.

In regard to Shelly's problem, Ted took the position that she was simply suffering growing pains and that the issue was being blown out of proportion. He refused to participate in psychotherapy.

Donna, the mother, attributed her daughter's symptoms to the stress of maintaining a B-plus average and adjusting to the transition from middle school to high school. She denied there being any serious problems within the family.

Early in therapy, I invited Shelly and Donna to embark on an imagery journey together. Simultaneously, they put themselves in a deeply relaxed state and I provided them with the following structure:

"Now, each of you sees the other clearly and you can really feel each other's presence as you begin to explore a house where you are being held prisoner. You don't know whose keeping you there or why—you just know you are locked in. The place is comfortable enough but somebody doesn't want you to get away.

"You're in the living room when you hear some sounds from beneath you. They are coming from the basement. You realize there is something or someone down there. You find the door to the basement. It is locked, but there is a key hanging beside it. What will you do?"

Donna responds quickly. "I'm sure it's someone who has come to rescue us. I'm going to open the door and call for help."

"Wait a minute, Mom," says Shelly, raising her hand in a halting motion. "I'm not so sure it's friendly. I feel scared. I think we ought to leave it where it is and look for another way out."

"Don't be silly. I'm opening the door."

(Pause.)

Shelly half whispers, "I see the door opening. It looks dark down there to me."

Donna seems surprised. "You're right. It's dark to me, too."

"Someone's coming up the stairs." The girl appears anxious. " I can see it now. It's some kind of ape."

"It looks more like a man to me. Well.....maybe half and half."

"I think it means to hurt us, Mom. Let's split."

"No. It is hurt. It's starting to fall down."

"Yes. I see it falling, but it's wild, Mom. Let's leave it."

"Shelly, you know I wouldn't leave any helpless creature. I'm getting some water to give it. Once it's revived, I'm sure it will help us."

"I don't know where it came from, Mom, but I see a kitty now and its telling me we're in a lot of danger. It says if we'll follow it upstairs, it will show us a way out."

"If it will make you feel better, go on. This creature is more man than just an ape and I'm going to help it. I assure you there is nothing to be afraid of."

"O.K., it's your funeral. I'll just go on my own. I'm following the cat up the stairs. It leads me to a ladder going to the attic.

"I climb up and the cat shows me a small window which is open. A tree branch touches the window, so I can climb out of it directly onto the tree. The kitty shows me how to do it. It's scary but I climb out and carefully make my way to the trunk of the tree. I climb down several branches but the bottom one is still pretty high off the ground.

"I decide to drop to the ground, but when I do I feel this sharp pain in my ankle. I'm afraid I've sprained it. I can't get up and walk." As she images this, Shelly winces as if in pain.

Donna's voice comes to life. "Hang on, honey, I'll be there in a minute. This man is waking up and he's big and strong enough to knock the door down. That's exactly what he's doing. He's knocking the door down and, now, I'm outside. I see you. I'm right with you. I'll help you up and we'll go home."

"Yeah. I can feel your arm around me." (Pause.) "I don't see the creature."

"I don't either. He's gone."

Their shared imagery ended as they returned safely to their own home. The follow-up session was bland with neither client reflecting much insight. Their mutual feeling was that the imagery had demonstrated their closeness and caring for one another.

A crisis arose some weeks later when Shelly, with newly increased ego strength, stated at our session that she did not like the way her father "played" with her. Donna was immediately flustered and angry, asking whatever did she mean by that.

"I feel like he's being flirty," said the girl. "He's all over me like some animal. Other fathers don't act like that - of course, other fathers aren't drunk most of the time, either."

The child probably did not realize she was completely blowing apart her mother's fantasy of their family life being free of problems. Donna began to scold her for saying "awful" things about her father. Soon, they were hurling invectives at each other.

Picking up on Shelly's referring to her father as an animal, I interrupted them, reminding Shelly that she had described the creature in their mutual imagery as being animal-like. The girl said she had known at the time that the ape-man was her father but had been afraid to say so because her mother is so protective of him.

She had sensed for some time that his behavioral controls were shaky and that there were sexual overtones in his so-called playfulness. Furthermore, even though her mother chose to close her eyes to it, Shelly suspected that Ted's nights out were not just with the boys.

The teenager expressed resentment regarding her mother's complacency about all of that and the way she doted on him when he was around. Just like in their imagery, she had tried to warn her mother of dangers, but the warning fell on deaf ears.

The girl called the kitten the "warm, fuzzy" part of herself (not realizing the Freudian implications of a pussy) that felt she should save herself. Donna hadn't seen the kitten at all, just as she had failed to notice her daughter's rapidly emerging sexuality.

It took Shelly much longer to see the meaning of falling from the tree and "hurting" herself. By the time she did, she had grown aware that her stomach pains were the same kind of protective, attention getting device. By being hurt, she could hook mom's Rescuer and also prevent herself from becoming too independent and aggressive.

Donna initially denied that the fantasy creature represented her husband but it started her thinking about it. She was more willing to accept the portrait of herself as a compassionate caretaker who would never leave the side of anyone who was down. As she started to apply this awareness to her relationship with both her husband and daughter, her inner insecurity surfaced and gradually she faced her rescuing motif as her insurance that she would not be abandoned.

As Donna became less of an enabler, Ted began to feel pressured to "grow up." He initially reacted to it with anger but, faced with the realistic possibility of losing his family, his own deep seated dependency needs surfaced. He became anxious and depressed and entered into treatment.

As with Donna and Shelly, those of us who dare to share the images which abide in the dark caverns of our mind often walk away from these experiences knowing more than we know we know. As we touch soul to soul we acquire not so much an answer as a bolder, more exciting question.

In "The Wasteland," T.S. Eliot (1934) writes of walking with another and counting only two persons but always being aware that yet another walks beside his companion. In our encounters with ourselves and others there is, indeed, always a third beside us. It is the messenger from our inner world. Just when we think we know each other, the third speaks and we realize we are meeting for the first time.

CHAPTER FOURTEEN

A FRIEND FOR LIFE

Were there but world enough and time to utilize only one imagery technique, the Inner Guide technique is easily the choice. It has been called the most powerful intervention in all of psychotherapy and I agree. It also has uses which extend beyond therapy.

The Inner Guide image has appeared in some form in various cultures throughout history. It began to receive renewed attention in psychotherapeutic literature in the 70's in the writings of Samuels and Bennett (1973), Irving Oyle (1976), and others.

The label which authors assign to the unconscious principle behind the image involved varies. Some of the more popular designations are the "inner physician or therapist," the "inner advisor" and the "inner guide," the term which I prefer.

Shamanic Origin of the Inner Guide

In Chapter Two, we alluded to the shamanic tradition which is the foundation of the entire field of therapeutic imagery. The Inner Guide technique epitomizes that world wide tradition.

The shaman, you may recall, is a sojourner in two worlds —the world of ordinary awareness and a "shadow world" inhabited by a variety of spirit entities. For the shaman, there is no strict division between these two worlds.

The shaman knows that spirits can disguise themselves as humans or can just as easily reside in plants, rocks, rivers, the wind or any other product of nature. Their possession of a real human being is regarded as the primary cause of illness.

Good health and good fortune depend on a balance and harmony between the ordinary world and the spirit world. Therefore, the shaman must be a constant traveler between the two worlds, mediating with the inhabitants of both.

From the modern, psychological viewpoint, the spirits with which the shaman interacts would be identified as projections of his inner unconscious forces and those of his clients. From the shaman's perspective, they are real inhabitants of a real, non-material universe. Whatever their true origin, the spirits serve to direct the action of the shaman and his followers.

The central experience in the shaman's life is his initiation. This may follow an apprenticeship under another shaman or may occur spontaneously. Under the latter circumstances, the initiatory phenomena are taken to mean that the person has been marked or chosen for the role of shaman.

The initiation may occur in a dream or during an illness but it is usually the phenomenon of an induced trance state. The essence of the experience is a long, dream-like journey through the underworld, culminating in a vision of heaven.

On this journey, the shaman meets a number of spirits, good, evil and neutral in nature. Some of them must be fought and defeated in order to proceed. Others assist him in magical ways. Often, they give the shaman certain objects that have magical powers. At the climax of the trip, an archetypal figure takes charge of the shaman's body, dismembering it and, then, restoring it.

Symbolically, the shaman has met death and been reborn, never again to be quite the same. He now has the powers of healing and prophecy and can communicate with the non-ordinary universe at will.

In parallel fashion, we seek our Inner Guide as an ambassador of the non-ordinary world, our unconscious mind. Our Twentieth Century sophistication tells us that the Guide is a product of right brain activity—that essentially it is a personification of a part of our nervous system. However, there remain many in this day and age who view the Guide as a manifestation of a true spirit akin to the guardian angel which some religions, notably Roman Catholic, teach children about.

I don't believe anyone can identify with absolute certainty the ultimate source of this imagery. Therefore, it is appropriate to accept and respect whatever interpretation the imagist assigns to it.

In *The Way of the Shaman*, Michael Harner (1982) informs us that the shaman has a particular guardian spirit or power animal that assists him in various ways. These animal spirits are always beneficial, putting their wisdom and strength at the shaman's disposal. The Inner Guide is cut from this mold.

The Nature of the Inner Guide

While the Inner Guide may take the form of any living entity, more often than not, it appears in the form of an animal. In this exercise, we, like the shamans, are in the position of talking with the animals who, in turn, can impart to us extraordinary knowledge and power.

The Inner Guide is our guiding light, wise, caring and non-judgmental. It knows, understands and accepts everything about us. Emanating from our unconscious, it is capable of employing all of our unconscious powers in helpful ways. Like our unconscious, it is not bound by earthly physics or the mechanics of the material universe. It is part of another reality.

Once we discover and accept our Inner Guide, we have made a friend for life. It will be an abiding presence unless we choose to ignore or abandon it. It will stick by us as long as we live.

On the mission to track down the Inner Guide, the Private Eye should expect the unusual. When Sherlock meets the Guide, he will be meeting himself expanded to his full potential.

Sherlock, the Private Eye, The Great Investigator—whatever we choose to call it—is one fragment of that intuitive, directive, transcendent, spiritual part of ourselves which can be called Higher Consciousness. The Inner Guide embodies all of these attributes. The first meeting is a moment to be remembered and revered.

For this reason, some special preparation for imaging the Inner Guide is customary. The imagist is advised that the Guide has been a functional part of her personality all along, but probably not the focus of her conscious attention.

Periodically, the client may have made contact with her Inner Guide but failed to identify it. This may have been when a quiet voice from within seemed to be urging the client to do or not do a particular thing. It may have been an "a-ha" experience when that same voice said, "I knew things were going to turn out this way." The Guide may have spoken comfortingly at a time of great stress or tragedy. Imagery will now allow the patient to have a conscious, working relationship with this wise and compassionate part of her self.

Some clients appreciate being oriented to the fact that working with the Inner Guide engages their less used right brain functions and, thus, constitutes a fresh approach to solving their problems. Those with self esteem problems are particularly gratified to discover that they have such a powerful, higher functioning component to what they have thought was an inferior personality.

Other more spiritually oriented clients like to draw parallels between their Inner Guides and the spirit guides of the Native Americans or Guardian Angels of Christianity. Some grasp the archetypal nature of the Guide. In practice, both religious and archetypal images (Jesus, the Virgin Mary, Saints, the Wise Old Man and Wise Old Woman) are forms taken by the Guide with some frequency.

The client should be reminded of the importance of accepting the Inner Guide in whatever form it takes, even if it seems inane or in some way distasteful. He is informed that the Guide will have gender and a name and should be treated with respect.

The Guide may show sensitivity to the fact that the client has been largely neglecting it throughout life and is now seeking it as a friend and helper. It may be skeptical of the client's sincerity and, judging by the number of people who abandon their Guides after a particular problem is resolved, the skepticism is justified.

Procedure for Contacting the Inner Guide

It is recommended that the client be prepared to ask the Guide for advice on some specific matter of concern at the time of the first meeting. The question should be formulated prior to beginning the exercise.

The procedure begins with relaxation. When the client is suitably relaxed, the therapist or helper can give the following instructions or they can be committed to an audio tape for those working alone.

"Now that you're relaxed, it's important to find a suitable setting in which to meet your Guide.....You can do this by allowing yourself to drift off right now to some setting out of doors that is pleasing to you.....It can be any setting you choose.....The beach.....On a mountain.....In the woods.....Or a meadow.....Any place you like as long as you feel at one with your surroundings....Let yourself be there right now....It's your own special place....Take in all of the sights, sounds, smells, sensations....As you do this, describe your experience out loud to me."

As usual, it is important to elicit enough description to ensure that the client has a sense of being truly present in her ideal setting. This accomplished, continue with the instructions.

"This is a wonderful place to meet your Guide....So, find a spot where you can stand, sit or lie down....Whatever is comfortable....Find that spot and get situated....This is where you will wait for your Inner Guide to appear....That's all you have to do....Just wait patiently....When something—anything—captures your attention, describe it to me....It can be anything, no matter how trivial it may seem....Until then, just enjoy your surroundings and wait quietly...

"I'll wait quietly with you....We'll both be quiet and patient."

At this point, therapist and client wait for the Guide to appear. Usually, the Guide arrives within a few seconds. Sometimes a longer wait is required. If so, it is important that the therapist not seem to be restless or to be pressuring the client to "get on with it." The tension thus created can only further impede the client's efforts.

The therapist should be vigilant for signs of eye movement as indicators that the client's imagery has intensified. When it is observed, the imagist can be asked what is happening. In the absence of such activity, the therapist can make a supportive comment every few seconds such as, "We're remaining calm as we watch and wait."

Before starting the exercise many clients express concern that no Guide will appear. At the workshops I've conducted, therapists express even greater concern about that posssiblity, wondering what they should do in that eventuality.

The situation does arise but not frequently. I will usually allow up to about ten minutes if the client is tolerating the time lapse well. At that point, I will suggest that enough time has been given to the exercise for the moment and that we shall repeat it at our next session, adding that Guides have minds of their own about timing and that we shall simply provide other opportunities for the Guide to appear.

I also alert the client to pay special attention to his dreams on the night of the session and make an effort to recall them. I have found many times that, when the Guide does not appear during the exercise, it will appear in a dream following the exercise.

Asked later in dialogue why they chose to come forth in a dream rather than during the imagery session, the Guides sometimes report that the patient was not sufficiently relaxed to tune in to their image in the office or that they have been contacting the patient in dreams all along or that the patient's negative attitudes or disbelief during the waking state were too strong and warded them off.

Chances are good that, by the second or third attempt, the Guide will appear. The therapist's patience and confidence seem to be essential elements. The therapist's willingness to stick with it helps the client to allay the fear and embarassment which are the main blocks. Should the client remain stuck, another treatment modality may have to be instituted.

Another concern of both clients and therapists is the appearance of negative Guides, those which take the form of things repulsive or frightening to the client. Snakes, which are a much misunderstood symbol and not necessarily negative at all, are one example of a form which many people find disturbing.

Once accepted and entered into dialogue with, this kind of Guide will often change form to a more positive image or it may educate the client into recognizing that it is not essentially negative. Guides that change form often acknowledge that they initially took the negative form in order to test the client's commitment and willingness to persevere.

The first contact with the Inner Guide may be a highly emotional experience. The majority of clients report an overwhelming feeling response which includes a measure of joy. Weeping and ecstatic expressions confirm this.

Joyful displays on the part of the Guide as well are frequently noted. The Guide may warmly embrace the client or dance with happiness at their meeting. Other Guides are more wary and stand-offish and may have to be coaxed to come close. These usually seriously doubt the sincerity of the client's intention to establish and maintain a relationship.

Once contact with the Inner Guide is made, it is important to elicit from the client a full description of the Guide. If she does not spontaneously do so, she should be directed to find out the Guide's name and gender and to thank him or her for appearing.

Following the introductory dialogue, the client should ask the advice of the Guide on the matter which was predetermined. The advice may or may not seem to be illuminating but the client is encouraged to accept whatever is offered and to thank the Guide for offering it. The advice unfailingly should be discussed in follow-up.

The exercise ends with the making of a definite and specific date for the next contact between Guide and client. This is likely to be the time of the next therapy session but it could be an "at home" meeting between sessions. In either case, it is extremely important that the date be kept. Guides take this to heart as a meaningful indication that the patient truly means business about a relationship.

In every follow-up of an Inner Guide imagery session careful attention should be paid to whatever advice is received. Advice obtained in this manner should not be acted upon blindly without rational consideration. The dangers are that it may be impractical, it may require considerable analysis to be correctly understood, it may be partial or it may be undecipherable.

On the other hand, most of the time the advice given will be straightforward, insightful and in the client's best interest. Even so, it deserves rational inspection before being put into action.

Should the client expect to encounter more than one Guide? Multiple Guides are the rule rather than the exception. Some Guides have specialized functions and are especially helpful with certain kinds of problems. At least one Guide of the opposite sex can be expected.

From the Therapist's Notebook: First Encounter

My heart was beating excitedly. The workshop leader had said it was time for us to meet our Inner Advisers. Based on the discussions preparatory to this event I fancied meeting a stately lion or a wisdom figure like Socrates.

I went to my special place and seated myself on the bank of my quiet, still pond. I was aware of animal life all around me and was filled with anticipation of one of these life forms suddenly invading my awareness to announce its identity as my Adviser. My prior imagery training allowed me to remain expectantly calm and patient.

Soon I found my gaze transfixed on the brownish pond water. I felt unable to raise my head and look around. A shuffling sound told me something was approaching.

I shifted my eyes to the left, the direction of the sound. I was surprised and, I must say, disappointed to find in my peripheral field of vision a pair of masculine feet encased in sturdy sandals. Surely I was not destined to have a Hippie Adviser.

Flexibility returned to my body and I was able to follow the feet upward. The person was clad in a coarse brown robe tied at the waist by a dirty strand of rope. The hood topping the robe was pulled up obscuring most of the face. Around the neck hung a heavy wooden cross about six inches in length.

No, I did not have a Hippie to contend with. I had a monk.

I sighed heavily as I asked if he were my Adviser. I had parted company with the Roman Catholic Church in my early adulthood and had no real enthusiasm about gettting a cleric of that persuasion for an Adviser. But the head nodded yes and I politely thanked him for coming.

I asked if he had a name and was puzzled when he didn't answer readily. I wondered if I had already managed to offend him with my negativism.

In a moment a vivid picture of an arrow in flight flashed before me. Somehow I knew that image represented his name.

I drew closer to him. "Arrow?"

The head nodded.

"Don't you talk?" I asked, my disappointment growing by the moment.

Another picture flashed. It was of Arrow and me. We were walking side by side along a road in silence.

It was clearly an answer to my question. I supposed that our communication was going to be limited to telepathically transmitted images.

I tried to conceal my thought that I had drawn a lenon for an Adviser. God forbid I should have gotten one easy to work with.

All of us at the workshop had prepared questions regarding some problem in our lives to present to our Advisers. I told Arrow I would like to give him mine and he nodded firmly.

His cowl obscured his features in a way that made it difficult to determine his age but I intuited he was about forty. I was to discover in subsequent contacts that his age and his features were subject to change.

Oh, how I would have preferred the unambiguous figure of an articulate Wise Old Man. I was having to work hard at accepting what I had been given.

I asked him about a client I was treating. I had been seeing her for a lengthy period of therapy and lately we seemed to be badly stuck. I wondered if I should terminate the therapy and/or refer her to someone else.

My inner screen lit up and I was shown a movie of myself at the foot of a wall, beginning to climb it via its rocky protuberances. I climbed and climbed but seemed to get nowhere nearer the top.

Although little clock time passed the movie seemed interminable. I reached a point of feeling totally spent and wanting to quit. Just as I thought of descending, the top was there and I was suddenly over. Arrow had pictorially instructed me to persevere.

Arrow's answer to that question and others that followed was on the order of a Cecil B. DeMille production but it was clear enough. I stayed with my client and we broke out of our rut in just two more sessions.

As I scheduled my next meeting with Arrow and bade him good-bye I had no idea he would become the valued companion he is today. I have even grown to appreciate his strictly non-verbal way of communicating.

After we had worked together for a while he informed me that he had taken a sacred vow of silence. This has turned out to be not so bad. He has taught me to respect the beauty and sanctity of silence.

Those of you meeting your Guides for the first time should be aware that it may not be so easy to drop the relationship once it has begun. Some Guides, Arrow included, have been known to pursue their hosts.

Shortly after my first meeting with him I started to ignore him on the grounds that my busy schedule left no time for imagery. Worse than ignoring him, I made a couple of dates to meet with him and broke them. My dominant Left Brain provided me with abundant rationalizations for not doing the exercise.

After I had ignored Arrow for several weeks a strange event transpired. While sorting through my day's mail, a brochure advertising occult reading materials caught my eye. Its cover was adorned with a pencil drawing of a monk and it looked just like Arrow. It was so like him that it startled me.

Immediately my thoughts returned to him and I resolved to take time out for an imagery session later that day. I failed to follow through.

The next day brought an even more remarkable occurrence. As I sorted through the mail the very same brochure grabbed my attention. Apparently my name had turned up twice on the publisher's mailing list. For me it was synchronicity, clear as day. I knew I *must* get in touch with Arrow. I told my secretary to leave me undisturbed for twenty minutes.

I imaged myself at my special place for imagery, the pond, and invited Arrow to appear. He was damn slow in coming. I expected him to be angry but he acted glad to see me. Communicating telepathically he showed me a picture of him mailing the two brochures.

The Elephant on the Sofa

Many people claim they are never quite the same after meeting their Guides. Those who work with their Guides on a continuing basis say that these "friends for life" become an integral part of their experience of reality.

Understandably, those who find their Guides to be a resource for healing, problem solving and transcendence sometimes want to communicate with others about them. This is not easy to do.

One of my clients, Harry, had told his wife that he was to meet his Inner Guide at his next therapy session. He treated the whole thing like a joke, commenting about my statement that he should behave respectfully toward his Guide.

After meeting his Guide, Umbriago, Harry was so caught up in the experience that when he came home that evening he promptly announced to his wife that he was retreating to his den to do some more communicating with this fascinating new entitty in his life. Filled with curiosity, the wife slipped into the room and remained unobstrusively quiet while Harry and Umbriago dialogued out loud.

The client concluded the session by offering Umbriago an imaginary peanut and telling him to stick it up his nose.

"My God," said the wife when the exercise was obviously over, "that's not very nice. I thought you said you were to treat your Guide with respect."

"I did," said the client. "He's an elephant."

His spouse was dumbfounded. It hadn't occurred to her that Advisers can be non-human.

"You mean there's an elephant on my sofa?" She eyed the piece of furniture warily.

"Yes."

"And you were talking with him?"

"Yes."

"Harry! I don't believe any therapist is telling you to do this!"

Harry's wife became so curious about his "craziness" that she eventually learned to communicate with her own Guide.

Descriptions do not do justice to the Inner Guide experience. This is why through the years it has been my practice to tape record many of the first meetings between clients and Inner Guides. The recordings capture the drama of the moment and give both patient and therapist an opportunity to savor and study it. Thereafter, I ask each client to keep a journal of his dialogues with the Inner Guide which take place outside of the therapy hour. From these primary sources, it has been possible to assemble a sampling which might be called an Inner Guide Parade.

My enthusiasm for the Inner Guide technique is so strong that most of my clients "catch" it before they set out to meet their Guide for the first time. This contagious positive attitude may account for the high rate of successful contacts. One of the drawbacks is that clients who have difficulty making contact with their Guides tend to suffer keen disappointment and/or anxiety.

The Case of the Hard to Find Guide

Lucy was a self sacrificing, attention starved, middle aged woman who felt abandoned by her now grown children and busy husband who was at the peak of his professional career. She genuinely looked forward to discovering her Guide and utilizing his or her wisdom to develop a plan for cultivating new interests and relationships.

Having loved the woodlands as a child, she invited her Guide to first come to her in a peaceful, shady forest. She sat on the ground with her back propped against the trunk of a massive oak and patiently awaited her Guide's arrival.

After just over a minute, she began to express concern that nothing was going to happen. I told her she had only been waiting a very short time and suggested she relax and remain alert to anything entering her awareness.

After four minutes had passed, I began to share some of her apprehension. I told her to look around and describe everything in her immediate environment.

She described the blue sky and the bright sun whose light filtered down through the branches of the tree. She noted green grass all around and the chirping of birds but nothing was vying for her attention. She verbalized that her Inner Guide had probably chosen to neglect her just like everyone else in her life.

She imaged herself closing her eyes for a brief nap. At that moment, a deep, masculine voice boomed, "I am here, Lucy!"

She popped her eyes open to see who was talking, but there was nothing in her visual field. I suggested she call out to her Guide and she did.

"Are you my Guide and, if so, where are you?"

The reply surprised her. "Damn it, Lucy, you're overlooking the obvious. I'm right here."

The woman appeared genuinely perplexed. "I don't see you. What's your name?"

"Mr. Oakley," came the response.

Then, it dawned on Lucy that she was engaged in dialogue with the comfortable, protective oak against which her back was pressed.

One might think that an oak tree would make a pretty constricted sort of Guide compared to an eagle, say, or a fox. Mr. Oakley turned out to be quite versatile. On his trunk was a door, invisible to the naked eye but which, when opened, led to out-of-this world places peopled by auxillary Guides who assisted Lucy in varied ways.

Mr. Oakley was also able to use his limbs like hands, sometimes lifting the patient up high. This had the effect of alleviating depression and helping her to see beyond her distress of the moment. He was instrumental in her development of an interest in (wouldn't you know) birds—a hobby she now thoroughly enjoys.

Lucy's experience points up the importance of being prepared for the Guide to appear in unlikely forms. I have joined people in working with Guides who appeared as a ball of fire, an ant, a mummy, Eve (of Genesis fame), a lobster, a Barbie doll and motley other characters. Most clients have little or no conscious awareness of why their Guide assumes its specific form. Many say their Guide did not turn out to be anything like what they would have expected.

The Case of the Long Lost Guide

For some individuals meeting the Guide is like a reunion with a long, lost friend. Jules first encountered his Guide, Corky, in a corn field. As he wandered through the rows of plants he spied Corky in the distance. As he drew nearer he kept saying, "I know him; I'm sure I know him."

The actual moment of recognition was joyous. Jules burst into tears and ran to embrace his old, dear friend.

When the greeting was completed he explained to me that Corky was his imaginary playmate, his constant companion during the lonely, childhood years when he was suffering much physical abuse. He had abandoned this one true friend when his mother told him she would send him away to a "crazy house" if he ever mentioned Corky again.

The Guide, a wise child, was every bit as enthusiastic over the reunion as Jules. He turned somersaults as he ran to greet his long lost buddy and climbed up on his back for a piggy-back ride after they hugged. Jules vowed to Corky that they would never be separated again.

Unfortunately, many people seek out their Guides at a time of crisis and appreciatively work with them until the problem is resolved, then start to ignore them or abandon them totally. The Guide, being an intrinsic part of the total personality remains on the scene but is relegated to the background where it will continue to function but without the zest and richness it contributes as a conscious co-participant in daily living. Consciously or unconsciously, our Guides are friends with whom we are destined to stick together for the the rest of our lives.

The Case of the Hideous Guide

Occasionally, Guides take on a form which is frightening or repulsive to the imagist. As in the case of Melanie, this may be the Guide's way of testing the patient's seriousness of intent.

Melanie was a bright, pretty young woman who for several years had been on again, off again in her struggle with drugs and alcohol. Prior to beginning therapy, she had episodically invested time and energy in self analysis and the pursuit of self-help programs.

Along the way, she had dabbled with the Inner Guide technique, contacting at one point a beautiful butterfly and, at another, a chimpanzee. After commiting herself to work with these images, she soon returned to her addictions and totally neglected them.

At our first session devoted to discovering her Inner Guide, Melanie sat beside a pool in a garden. To her horror, an eel, crackling and sparking with electrical charges, slithered toward her from the pool. Too frightened to run, she remained immobilized as the animal announced that her name was Medusa.

Melanie wanted to send the eel away. She said, if that was her Guide, we could all just forget it. She declared Medusa potentially hurtful and was not about to get hurt in order to get well.

At that point, Medusa crawled back into the water and the patient returned to ordinary consciousness. In our follow-up, I reminded her of her statment about not being willing to get hurt in order to get well. I suggested that this attitude reflected not just her problem with her Guide, but also her basic problem in regard to her addictions. She was not willing to endure the pain necessary to recovery.

We agreed that accepting the possibility of enduring discomfort in working with her Guide might somehow break the ground for her to get through the pain of becoming well. She went back to her pool for another meeting with Medusa and, this time, the eel was even more highly charged with electricity. It crawled toward her aggressively, stopping just in front of her. When she said she wanted to be friends, it hissed at her.

I asked Melanie if she would take the risk of putting out her hand to it and she reluctantly agreed. Her hand trembled as she extended it before her. Gritting her teeth, she made contact.

What occurred next was one of those miracles of imagery. Melanie felt a tingle rather than a shock and saw Medusa fly through the air back into the pool where she was instantly transformed into a beautiful, friendly dolphin.

Coco, the dolphin, revealed in dialogue that she had first appeared as the eel in order to test the depth of Melanie's motivation. The client's willingness to make contact in spite of all the threatening attributes was the clincher. Coco was now agreeable to assuming executive duties as Inner Guide. She reminded her host that a certain butterfly and chimp were also standing by to help out.

Melanie embarked on her journeys in the shaman's world with three guides already in place. As noted earlier, this phenomenon of multiple guides is commonplace. Each may offer some specialized service or maintain a specific viewpoint different from the others. It is also possible that there will be little differentiation between them.

The Case of the Prophetic Guide

Coley was surprised and annoyed when he asked his Guide for advice about relocating from Florida to Texas. He had come to trust Bascom the Owl to deliver wise counsel on almost any matter. This time, Bascom said flatly, "I don't know."

I suggested that Coley ask his Guide if he knew anyone who could supply some advice and he replied affirmatively. Bascom then instructed Coley to follow him on what turned out to be a rather long hike up a mountain. Coley knew he was being taken to an inner landscape he had never before visited. At the top of the mountain, they came upon a simple hut.

Bascom prodded Coley to enter the dwelling. It was dark inside, but gradually his eyes adjusted and he found himself in the presence of an Old Man with a beard, wearing animal skins. Somehow, he knew that the Old Man had no eyesight, yet he sensed that the wise one could "see" things far beyond the capabilities of ordinary mortals.

Coley made his request for advice and endured some long moments of silence while the old man engaged in comtemplation. At last, he spoke.

"It is good you have come to me," he said, "for there are twists and turns on the path ahead of which you have no knowledge. All of the signs are positive for you to go away, yet Fate says 'no.' More than you know, you are needed where you are. Stay."

In our follow-up, we discussed that there was no solid evidence to back up what the Old Man had said and that, in the absence of such, it seemed acceptable for Coley to go ahead and accept his new job offer if he found it appealing. He decided to think about it.

Next day, the patient called to say he was turning down the offer. He really believed some prophetic part of himself had spoken.

Three months later, Coley's father died suddenly and unexpectedly. Within a few weeks, his mother suffered an emotional breakdown requiring hospitalization. His presence in the area was sorely needed.

Was this the fulfillment of the old man's prophecy? I don't know, but Coley has no doubt of it.

Do Guides ever give bad advice? In the sense of maliciousness, I have not found this to be so. However, some Guides fail to sufficiently take into account reality factors and, on that basis, may give advice that is inappropriate in the light of the patient's circumstances and/or resources.

The Case of the Incoherent Guide

There may also be occasions on which Guides offer advice which is unintelligible or, at least, undecipherable. This is why the follow-up evaluation of each imagery session is so important.

Liane had for a Guide a bear named Betsy who was full of love and compassion and who taught her host to be a more open, affectionate person. However, when it came to advice, Betsy was a bust, at least we assume so, because her advice could never be understood.

For example, when Liane asked Betsy for advice concerning her developing relationship with an attractive new man in her life, Betsy said, "You have found something from your past which you no longer need but which, if pursued, can lead you to a map of future ruins."

After getting a few samples of this kind of response, I requested that Liane ask Betsy if she was serious or just bullshitting. Betsy assured us she was serious and that she could make things no clearer.

Liane explained to Betsy that she appreciated her efforts but that she needed a source of more intelligible information. She asked if there were a Guide available who specialized in clear advice and the bear acknowledged that there was. Soon Liane was working with a parrot named Lola in addition to Betsy. Lola was articulate and clear.

Symptom Removal

One of the most astounding powers of the Inner Guide is its ability to provide temporarily complete relief from pain and other symptoms. This phenomenon has been reported in the literature (Bresler and Trubo, 1979; Jaffe and Bresler, 1980) and can be demonstrated by having the client ask the Inner Guide if she has the power to allow the client to experience a few moments of total freedom from symptoms.

If the Guide says "yes," you can proceed immediately. If the response is negative, find out from the Guide if there is another Guide who can make this possible and proceed from there.

It is truly amazing to see clients with chronic symptoms enjoying those few seconds of relief. Sometimes, it takes them a while to realize that it was they themselves who provided that relief. Just knowing that they have within them that power provides a tremendous incentive for further therapeutic work.

From the Therapist's Notebook: Second Guide

One day I asked Arrow if I had other Guides. He held up five fingers. I was sorry I had asked.

I requested to know if he thought it was the right time for me to meet any or all of them. He nodded, raising one finger. Somewhat relieved I asked him to take me to the one.

Arrow led me to a beach where a solitary oldtimer clad only in baggy Bermuda shorts was busy patching up a battered rowboat just a short distance from the shoreline. His head was crowned with sparse white hair which the stubble on his face matched exactly. His skin was tough and looked sun baked but his eyes were as blue as the sea. He saw us and waved.

"Who are you?" I asked as we drew near.

"Name's Jeremiah," he responded in a raspy voice. "Been expecting you."

"What do you want of me?" I questioned in accordance with the best therapeutic protocol.

"Sonny," he said patronizingly, "I've got the answers. I guess it's more a question of what you want of me."

"The answers to what?" I inquired densely.

"Son, I'm a prophet." His irritation with me was apparent. "I can tell you what's ahead."

"Like Jeremiah in the Bible?" I asked sceptically.

"The same." He took a little bow.

"Can you show me something of my future now?" I wanted to challenge him.

"Why not?" He flipped the little rowboat over.

"Hop in," he invited.

The craft did not look seaworthy to me. "Shouldn't we put it in the water first.?" I wanted to see if it would sink.

Jeremiah's neck reddened visibly. "Wise up, Sonny. This is no ordinary rowboat."

Beginning to like his crusty manner, I got into the boat. Jeremiah took the oars and to my astonishment the boat began to climb into the stratosphere.

"This little rig goes on land, air, sea or outer space," he said proudly.

Feeling insecure, I turned and waved to Arrow who was growing smaller by the second. We climbed steadily and rapidly and were soon in outer space.

It was an eerie trip. The silence of space was gigantic.

The little boat propelled itself along. Unlike in my flight with Aeneas I experienced no rush of wind. It was like floating in nothingness. Huge chunks of rock riding invisible waves drifted past us. The beautiful blue earth became grapefruit size. The other planets loomed larger.

"Where are we headed?" I asked hesitantly.

Jeremiah gave no reply. I figured I must have the least talkative guides in the entire history of imagery.

Soon it was apparent that we were headed toward a particular orb. I recognized massive craters. We were bound for the Moon.

The boat landed smoothly and I took in the landscape made familiar by the astronauts' photographs.

"Why are we here?" I asked.

"It's your future," the old man said. "It's yours."

I thought his symbolism was overwrought. "You mean I can have the moon?"

"That's right," said Jeremiah emphatically.

"That's very nice," I said feeling awkward.

"All you have to do," he continued, " is take care of what's buried here." He drew an X in the sands of the lunar landscape with his heel.

Next thing I knew, he handed me a shovel and I started to dig. I had soon uncovered a metal chest.

I opened the chest and found it full of pictures. To my surprise they turned out to be photographs from my childhood days. I recognized Sad Child, Scared Child, Hurt Child.

"What are these doing here?" I asked.

"You brought them with you," said the old beachcomber. "Here you are on another world and you brought that stuff with you."

"But I don't want them," I said angrily.

Jeremiah sniffed to clear his nose. "You'll have to do better than that. They're just as much heirs to the Moon as you are. You'll have to find a place for them."

"I thought I had," I said wearily.

"You just put them in a dark hole." I knew there was wisdom in his words. "They want to live along side of you."

Jeremiah continues to appear whenever some future

oriented issue has to be dealt with. He is not very patient with my slowness to catch on to things. Also he is greatly inclined to be sarcastic.

"I'm way ahead of you," he says. "Way ahead of you."

The Origin of Inner Guide Power

When all is said and done, we are still left with the question: what is the power of imagery and where does it come from? Who is this Guide who seems so different from any other part of me?

Our Guides are non-ordinary entities. They are our link between two realities: the material universe and the spiritual domain. They are helpful precisely because they are a mystery to us.

When Mr. Oakley admitted Lucy through that door in his trunk she entered a world where she learned much about the importance of being rooted in Mother Earth and the joys of sheltering and protecting creatures more vulnerable than herself. Is this not part of the lesson which the trees have to teach us all? Is it not ancient wisdom? By exactly what process did Lucy gain access to it?

When Jules met Corky in the cornfield, he experienced a sense of renewal and fulfillment. Was he really united with a part of himself that had been lost to him? Do all of us in the course of growing up fragment and sacrifice aspects of our personalities? If so, can we reclaim them as Jules seemed to do?

And what of Melanie who had to slay her own monster by embracing it? Once she accomplished this, she was shown the clean, sleek, pure environment of the dolphin and began to remove herself from the toxic environment of alcohol and drugs she had previously chosen. Is this an example of a power animal leading the way just as they have done for the shamans through the centuries?

Coley's wise old man seemed to be clairvoyant. Coley is convinced that such powers naturally reside within his higher consciousness. He walks closely with Bascom the Owl and the other Guides he has discovered. He claims his relationship with them has improved the quality of his life tremendously. Can this be and, if so, what is at work here?

The answer is wizardry. L. Frank Baum described it perfectly in *The Wizard of Oz*.

"You see, Oz is a Great Wizard, and can take on any form he wishes. So that some say he looks like a bird; and some say he looks like an elephant; and some say he looks like a cat. To others he

appears as a beautiful fairy, or a brownie, or in any
other form that pleases him......"

This wizardry is inherent in every human being's make-up.
It is magical but has nothing to do with the illusionary process we
commonly call magic. It is a gift of Nature which deserves our
respect and interest.

If you are making contact with your Inner Guide to
establish an ongoing relationhsip for learning and healing, it is
wise to think in terms of a life long commitment. Be prepared to ask
the questions which Walt Whitman asked in *Leaves of Grass*. Will
you give me yourself? will you come travel with me?

Shall we stick by each other as long as we live?

CHAPTER FIFTEEN

THE FARTHER REACHES

Many of us who work with imagery develop a sense of it being an awesome force which can affect our inner and outer worlds in many ways. This is said with the realization that no one has come close to unleashing its full potential. It seems to be capable of benefitting us in so many parameters of life that a single volume such as this cannot begin to catalogue the possibilites.

The foregoing material has presented in some depth the particular imagery techniques which I favor in my clinical practice but there are many more clinical as well as non-clinical uses of imagery. In this chapter, I shall attempt to highlight some of the directions toward which it is being researched and/or employed.

Imagery and Memory

Among its other functions, imagery has been demonstrated to be an aid to memorization. It is one of the ways by which the human nervous system stores information naturally and spontaneously. That function can be elaborated upon to improve and increase memory skills.

For example, one way to facilitate commiting to memory a list of words is to endow each word with high imagery value by creating vivid visual connections, the more outlandish the better. To remember ostrich, soldier, handkerchief and tree, one might entertain images of the ostrich with a military man on its back who is blindfolded with a handkerchief and they all plow into a coconut palm.

A similar principle is involved in what is known as the Method of Loci. In this approach, one recalls lists of objects by taking an imaginary walk through one's house and placing the objects to be recalled in specific spots.

Applying it to a grocery list, one might open the front door and see the rolls "roll" out onto the walk. In the living room, a milk cow is reclining on the sofa, drinking a cola while watching a Chiquita Banana ad on television, etc.

Used this way, imagery has the effect of making a dull list of words interesting and, therefore, more memorable. In fact, some things committed to memory via this method are difficult to forget.

Imagery and Athletic Skills

Daredevil stuntman, Evel Kneivel, was famous for roaring his motorcycle up a ramp, soaring over as many as seventeen parked cars and landing on the other side. His stunts were truly astounding.

When interviewed before the television cameras, Kneivel revealed that he used visualization as preparation for his astounding jumps. He would make a point of imaging himself leaving the ramp, flying through the air and landing on the other side.

For Kneivel and others who engage in physical acts requiring unusual strength, skill or coordination, imagery apparently acts as a sort of neurological programming for all the aspects of their mind/body system which will be involved in the performance of their feats.

In recent years, athletes from many different fields of sport have incorporated imagery into their training and preparation programs. Many maintain a strong belief that it improves their performance. They devote considerable time to developing visualizations of themselves performing at their best. These images are repeated until they become a behavioral reality.

In a more specialized mode, some athletes might image a particular animal whose attributes they need, such as a tiger for aggressiveness, a cheetah for fleetness, a gazelle for jumping, etc. Like the cave people of so very long ago, they are establishing a spiritual connection with the animal in order to share in its powers.

Energy release, a very important factor in sports performance, may also be subject to some degree of regulation through imagery. For example, an athlete may visualize a vial of adrenalin exploding inside of himself at the moment requiring his maxiumum output.

The Power of Positive Thinking

People in various walks of life have borrowed the athletes' idea. Many business and professional people image achieving the status to which they aspire or the realization of their definition of success.

In its most simplistic form, this practice is defined as positive thinking. Positive thoughts are said to attract positive responses from the external environment. Carried to its ideal conclusion this means that by consistently imaging having the kind of automobile you desire, the amount of money you want to make or even the kind of companion you long for, these things will come to you.

Of course, it is foolish to think that images alone will bring these things home. Active energy must also be directed toward attaining that which is desired.

Along the same lines, imagery is seen as a means of enhancing the process of becoming the kind of person you wish to be. If you wish to be thin, visualize yourself minus the excess poundage. If you wish to be more outgoing, picture yourself being friendly and sociable. Affirmations aimed at improving self esteem such as, "I am a valuable, worthwhile person," seem to have more potency when coupled with a positive visualization of one's self.

Imagery is used to rehearse scenarios of anticipated important encounters such as a job interview, a request for a raise or asking for a first date with someone wonderful. The person who has throroughly rehearsed a situation in this manner can approach the reality with confidence, knowing exactly what she intends to say and do. This is a particularly helpful practice for non-assertive people.

Madison Avenue is eager to have all of us view their clients in a positive light. Advertising experts study images carefully in regard to their impact on the public's buying attitudes. All of us are aware of how effective they are because we find ourselves replaying in our minds. often accompanied by jingles, many of the advertising images presented to us on television and in layouts.

Medical Applications of Imagery

The role of imagery in recovery from a variety of medical conditions deserves and has been given special attention. Gerald Epstein (1989), a psychiatrist who specializes in imagery work, has compiled a volume of imagery exercises called *Healing Visualizations: Creating Health Through Imagery*. It prescribes a variety of specific images formulated to heal specific physical and emotional disorders. The book is recommended as prime example of the medical approach to imaging.

What we call disease can be brought about by invasive microbes, injuries, the deterioration or malfunctioning of any part of the mind/body system, or social, emotional or mental distress. Once disease is firmly entrenched, it takes the concerted effort of the entire bio-psycho-socio-spiritual organism to dislodge it. If it is severe, much time and much repair may be required.

Those who have known profound, debilitating illness aptly describe recovery as an up-hill road. The toll is patience and perseverance, required at a time of low energy and lack of confidence. On this road, we are not privileged to enjoy a guarantee of reaching our desired level of functioning. Yet, there is a compelling force within each of us, no matter how sick we may be, to strive for wellness.

If you are recovering from an illness that is primarily physical, a basic goal is likely to be the stopping, reversing or limiting of tissue damage. Quite possibly, the treatment regimen prescribed by your doctor to achieve that goal can be enhanced by imagery techniques.

For example, imagery can be coupled with every dose of medicine you take. Depending on the intended effect of the medicine, the imagery should be focused on giving its operational components some form in your mind's eye.

If the drug is intended to stop infection, you might picture the medicinal ingredients as wild animals, aggressive creatures, gobbling up the alien invaders in your body. If it is to reduce inflammation, you could entertain images of little men whitewashing the area with a cooling, soothing lotion.

Be inventive. Choose visualizations which are meaningful and appealing to you regardless of the symbols someone else might use.

These same principles can be applied to the body's natural healing mechanisms. If your heartbeat is irregular, image it beating in time with some steady, rhythmic action. If blood vessels are constricted, image them becoming dilated and allowing a smooth, effortless passage for the blood. If you're asthmatic, take yourself imaginally to a mountain top and breathe deeply the cool, crisp, dry air.

Is there hard evidence that such techniques are effective? Not an abundance.

Do many people subjectively experience such techniques as effective? Yes.

In the literature, there are reliable accounts of imagery

being used to control heart rate and blood pressure levels. Alterations in the chemistry of the body and the enhancement of healing from wounds or surgical procedures through imagery has also been documented and, as we have already noted, it is recognized as effective in the regulation of pain.

One of the most effective imagery techniques for pain relief involves visualizing one of the hands being placed in a pail of cold, anesthetizing liquid. The hand feels immediately cold and, gradually, more and more numb. In a short time, it is completely without feeling.

The hand is then removed from the pail and brought to rest at the area of pain where the coldness and numbness is allowed to drain out of the hand into the painful area. When the transfer is complete, the pain spot is completely anesthetized.

Another kind of pain relieving imagery, effective for some people, is accomplished by visualizing the pain at its source of origin, be it the head, the back or any other part of the body. The pain is seen to be transmitting an electric-like current which travels to the brain, calling the brain's attention to the area of discomfort. Various switches along the route from the pain site to the brain are imaged. One by one, these are imaged to be shut off and there is a diminution of pain as each switch is thrown.

The Case of the Golden Bird

Anita was a young woman who faced having to live with a certain amount of lower back pain emanating from an inoperable condition. Her peak period of pain was in the evening, after her work day. She was aware that her job kept her distracted from the pain while at home she had more time to focus on it.

Over a short period of time, Anita constructed the most beautiful, appealing fantasy she could imagine. It involved being in a gorgeous, color splashed garden with a huge, blue-water pool fed by a fountain shooting high into the air. The most fascinating inhabitant of the garden was a bird the color of bright, shiny gold.

Anita worked out an agreement with the bird that, whenever she became caught up in her pain, the bird would appear and guide her to her garden. This became an automatic occurence which never failed to distract her from her discomfort. She simply could not be aware of her pain and all that beauty at the same time.

The Case of the Gastric Firemen

Lorna was a middle aged patient troubled by chronic indigestion. Her family affectionately teased her by calling her the Maalox Kid.

She learned to image the first pangs of indigestion as fire

alarms and visualized her body sending out little firemen in response. When they arrived on the scene, they sprayed foam on the excess acid and quickly dried it up. Then, they cooled the stomach down by rinsing it with cool water from their hoses.

With practice, Lorna began to achieve immediate relief from her indigestion with this imagery alone. She is no longer the Maalox Kid.

From the Therapist's Notebook: 120 Over 70

On Sunday I took my case of flu to the Walk-In Clinic. They gave me medication for my sore throat and told me my lower count was 110—too high. They instructed me to monitor my blood pressure.

I secured a monitor and began making regular checks. Part of the problem must have been the flu because I did not continue to get readings above 100. However, they did remain in the high 80's and low 90's.

I began to watch my diet and curtailed my salt intake. I decided to augment these measures with imagery and spent part of my habitual imagery time focusing on the reading I desired: 120/70.

After concentrating on those numbers for a few seconds I pictured my blood vessels dilating, allowing my blood to circulate smoothly and effortlessly throughout my body. I visualized the heart pump having to exert very little pressure as the river of blood flowed unimpeded. Finally, I imaged this free flowing circulation as having a relaxing effect on all the systems of my body.

Almost immediately, readings right after the imagery were near normal. Readings taken randomly at other times began to reflect a generalized lowering. Presently the top count registers 120 to 130 most of the time. The lower count is seldom above 80,

Psychiatric Applications of Imagery

If you are recovering from an illness that is manifested primarily as an emotional disturbance, the process may be expedited by having frequent images of and dialogues with your Tense Self, Depressed Self, Anxious Self, etc. By talking to them from your rational, Adult Self, you can act very much as a therapist, giving support, reinforcing insights and helping with problem solving. You can also put the dysfunctional part of yourself in touch with your Inner Guide to answer questions or deal with matters about which you are unsure.

The neuroses generate a tendency to endlessly review thoughts, feelings and images that are negative and frightening.

When you are aware of doing this, it is helpful not only to consciously direct yourself to stop but also to replace negative images with positive ones such as a trip to your special place or the reexperiencing of some happy occasion in your life.

Rosalind, who suffered from panic attacks, discovered as she worked with color imagery that visualizing the color green had an extraordinarily soothing effect on her.

She was most prone to panic states when in the car alone. Many times, she had found it necessary to pull off the road until her anxiety subsided.

This client bought herself a bright green scarf and began carrying it in the car with her wherever she went. By pressing the scarf against her racing heart, she could begin to calm down. The scarf also triggered images of green fields and green trees which had a calming effect on her.

When self confidence and self esteem are problems, the technique of visualizing the person you are becoming can be an antidote. See yourself as your "Best Self," you at your fullest potential, looking, feeling, acting the way you really want to be. Dialogue with that part of yourself; ask it for helpful tips; become that part of you and spend some time experiencing your world through his eyes.

Hugh was repulsed when he first imaged his Depressed Self. "Is that me?" he queried. "For Christ's sake! I look so woebegone and helpless. I hope that's not how people see me when I'm depressed."

Hugh soon concluded that the image accurately approximated his depressed countenance and announced that this realization left him more depressed than ever. He was glad to get in touch with his "Best Self" but was disappointed when that aspect suggested that he put on an act of feeling better than he did.

"That's phoney," he said. "Being phoney isn't going to help."

When his Guide, a frog named Gondolfo, backed up the "Best Self's" advice, Hugh decided to give it a try. For a few days, he grumbled about the uselessness of it all but, soon, he began to feel better. He learned that *acting* better can, indeed, result in *feeling* better.

The Case of the Runaway Tire

The technique of symptom imagery was delineated in an earlier chapter. It can be used during recovery to learn from more minor, secondary symtpoms as well as the major ones.

Gavin was in the process of recovering from a major depression and was making good progress. Imaging had become a regular feature of his recovery program.

After several months of therapeutic work, he found himself drifting back into his workaholic ways and noticed a marked increase in tiredness and irritability. He allowed his tired-ness to take form and a flat tire appeared.

Gavin proceeded to attach a hand pump to the tire and exerted a mighty effort to blow it up but it wouldn't budge. He then decided to remove it from the car and, just as he pulled it off, it began rolling away from him. He gave chase until the tire rolled onto the beach and into the surf. He swam after it, finally catching hold.

It was as he floated with the tire in the water that he noticed how peaceful and relaxing it was. He felt a strong urge to just continue drifting along that way indefinitely.

The next week-end, Gavin brought home no work from the office. Instead, he and his family took off for Ichnetucknee Springs and spent the day tubing. He returned rested and relaxed.

Application of Imagery to Addictions

No one knows the up-hill road better than the 15% of Americans who are chemically dependent. Chemical dependence is a disease which is chronic, progressive and terminal, if not treated. To further complicate the situation, the dependency can and often does exist side by side with other medical and psychiatric conditions.

In spite of frequently tragic consequences, substance abuse is often presented as an exciting and sophisticated activity in literture, music, theater and films. Among young people, addictions are often romanticized through stories of their entertainment idols getting hooked and/or unhooked. Such accounts appear with regularity in the media, sometimes in a glamourized form.

Those seriously striving to recover from an addiction know what an unglamorous, serious business it is. They also know it is a matter of life and death.

Lists of outstanding public personalities make a striking testimonial to the lethality of chemical dependence. Stephen Foster, W.C. Fields, Judy Garland, Montgomery Clift, Lenny Bruce, Marilyn Monroe, Jimi Hendrix, Janis Joplin and John Belushi are but a few of the names which come easily to mind. The up-hill road was too steep for them.

The first step in treatment is detoxification. Following it, the client is faced with the lengthy process of developing a balanced pattern of living in abstinence from mood altering substances. Usually, this involves a revamping of almost every area of life. Psychologically, giving up the substance takes on the dimensions of giving up everything familiar and enjoyable.

Since the majority of chemically dependent patients grew up in homes where one or more adults were also chemically dependent, their Inner Child was programmed or scripted by what they observed and felt during their developmental years. No matter how awful the situation, the lessons were there and the vulnerable Child could not help but record them:

"This is life, kid. This is how grown-ups act. This is how people treat each other. This is how you deal with feelings. This is what you can expect from other people."

Over and over the lessons were taught. Even as the Child vowed that she would be different, the lessons sank in. The process of growth and maturing allowed other parts of the personality to develop but the Inner Child remained the same.

Obviously, work with that Inner Child is crucial to the task of maintaining freedom from addiction. The negative programming of the Child and its relatively uncontrolled dominance over other aspects of the personality are key factors to be addressed in recovery. Therefore, Inner Child imagery is a useful tool for reprogramming and taking charge of the Child.

The Case of the Laughing Child

Warren was an alcoholic who, prior to going through detox, had handed his wife one of his golf clubs and defied her to hit him with it. Totally distraught, the woman complied. Ten stitches were required in Warren's head.

Later, Warren and I were working in therapy. He had completed a twenty-eight day withdrawal program and was attending AA regularly. He was concerned about the self destructiveness of his Inner Child and brought it up in dialogue with his imaged cowering little boy.

"Why did you ask Sally to hit you?" he queried.

To Warren's horror, the child laughed hysterically in response.

"Do you think it's funny?" he asked incredulously.

"Sure," said the Kid, "I thought it would be o.k. if she killed us." He was still giggling.

"Why did you think that?"

"Because she was about to leave. You weren't paying

attention but I could tell. She was going to walk out on us, sure as shooting. You didn't do anything to stop her but I did. I figured if she was going to leave we might as well be dead."

Warren sighed wearily, beginning to see the light. "You were remembering the time momma left us, weren't you?"

"Oh, yes,I always remember that," said the kid. "She went away and left me all alone with Daddy. I didn't think she was ever coming back. He was lying on the couch drunk and I was playing on the floor right beside him just to be close to someone.

"All of a sudden, he started puking and choking. He choked so bad and I didn't know what to do. He was turning blue. (Starts crying.) I started shaking him and he hit me. Then, he choked some more and blood started coming out of his mouth. He would have died if momma hadn't come back."

"And you think something equally dreadful will happen if Sally leaves?"

"Yes."

"And you'd rather die than be abandoned and helpless that way again?"

"Yes."

This encounter with his Inner Child enabled Warren to know, for the first time in more than just an intellectual way, the deep dependency that his outward behavior and attitude generally belied. From that point, he began to work on nurturing his frightened, needy Inner Child.

Worst Scenario Imagery can be put to good use when the urge to indulge in an addictive substance arises. Such urges are usually accompanied by pleasurable images of being part of a group, having "fun," being confident and carefree, being sexy and unhibited, etc. Taking a drink or getting a fix symbolizes a return to the excitement of the "good old days."

Such imagery becomes a positive reinforcer of the forbidden impulse. By creating a Worst Scenario Image, the positive reinforcement is quelled and aversive stimuli are substituted for it.

The Case of the Substitute Image

Lucas very successsfully used imagery as an intervention when he found himself entertaining pleasant fantasies about returning to his cocaine habit. He learned to immediately replace the positive images with images of being busted.

He conjured up vivid pictures of being arrested and going through the booking procedure. Having been through this in real life, he was able to capture all of the unpleasant aspects of it.

The client intentionally made the scenario even more horrible than anything he had actually experienced. He imaged his seven year old daughter walking in on him just as he was doing a line of coke. He imaged investing so much money in his drug habit that his family was deprived of necessities, losing their home and other possessions. He imaged behaving irresponsibly while under the influence and catching herpes or AIDS. By relentlessly substituting the Worst Scenario over a period of time, he found it increasingly difficult to identify a return to his habit as anything but a disaster.

Future Applications of Imagery

Interesting clinical work is being done in the relatively uncharted areas of imaging conception (Stokes and Stokes, 1986), birth (Grof, 1988) and death (Sheikh, Twente and Turner,1979). These are fairly new areas which should, when thoroughly explored have broad application in treatment and psychospiritual development.

The discovery that the human immune system is responsive to imaged messages presents the possibility that in the future imagery may play an increasingly important role in the treatment of various diseases including cancer. As previously noted, it is already being widely used and is gaining acceptance with medically trained professionals. It is part and parcel of the treatment modalities employed by the new field of medicine called psychoneuroimmunology.

Look for the Inner Guide technique to play a prominent part in all of the treatment applications just noted. It is innately wise in regard to the needs of the body and has access to the full power of the mind. It is equally wise in the methods and effects of prayer and meditation. These two kinds of wisdom render the Inner Guide consummately capable of facilitating healing of body, mind or soul. Guides can and will be called upon to give disease sufferers instruction, solace and alleviation of symptoms.

CHAPTER SIXTEEN

MADNESS AND HOLINESS

When I present workshops on therapeutic imagery, I find that many people, therapists as well as clients, find imagery frightening. When asked why, they start out with vague reasons but, usually, the bottom line is that it brings them too close to their concept of craziness. Haven't we heard all of our lives that hallucinations are a sure sign of schizophrenia and that those who talk to themselves are nuts?

The populous at large no longer views mental illness as the product of demon possession. People with very little education recognize that "crazy" people have lost control of their thoughts and behaviors. Their personality has disintegrated to the point that they are no longer functioning like a whole, unified person.

Herein lies the basic fear of imaging. It is a procedure which fragments us. Even so, it differs from psychosis in that consciousness of the imaging process is maintained throughout.

No matter how caught up in the imagery one may be, the inner observer remains aware. No matter how vivid or involving the imaged world may be, that part of the imagist does not lose sight of the fact that the body in the chair with the eyes closed continues to exist.

The fragmentation inherent in imagery is used paradoxically to facilitate integration of the personality. When I allow a particular component of my personality (Angry Me, Frightened Me, Playful Me, etc.) to manifest itself in some imaginary form, I am immediately in the position of giving it recognition and, as I interact with it, I am granting it the status of being an important and worthwhile part of me, even if troublesome. This is a far cry from declaring it unfit for conscious examination and suppressing it.

Psychotic people encounter some aspect of themselves without awareness that they are doing so or conscious desire to do so. Thus, they experience that part of themselves as an other who is actually present in the external world.

My interaction with my projected image is on an "as if" basis. I act as if it exists in the outer world, though my observer is not fooled by my action. Thus, there are never less than three components of myself doing imagery: the executive, rational self; the projected self (the image), and the observer.

There is no cause for alarm. These various aspects of the personality are called ego states. We all have them.

Our ego states make up that entity we like to think of as our solid self. That entity is actually more a patchwork of sub-selves, some of which are more tightly interlaced than others. Those which are least integrated are probably on the periphery because they are aggregates of attributes with which, for one reason or another, the executive does not wish to identify.

This means that all of our inner selves are not in agreement and that those of which we most disapprove are relegated to the status of Shadow, a dark side which is disowned. We do not want to bring our Shadow into the light.

This is what makes imagery so risky, so scary. It either pointedly invites some Shadow aspect to come into the light or makes it possible for this to happen spontaneously by virtue of our withholding the usual restrictions imposed by the left brain.

The risk is that we shall discover something horrible about ourselves. The fear is that we shall be powerless to deal with it.

The gain is that we shall expand our self awareness and become whole persons by facing and integrating our sub-selves as fully as possible. This principle is at work in the Jungian technique called Active Imagination, in Eric Berne's Transactional Analysis, in Fritz Perls' Gestalt Therapy , and in Assagioli's Psychosynthesis.

John and Helen Watkins (1979) were the first to describe a technique called Ego State Therapy. In their approach, under hypnosis, a client's various ego states are called forth and engage in dialogue with the therapist as if they were separate individuals.

From the Therapist's Notebook: Sub-selves

Imagery has made my various sub-selves so much more real to me. My dialogues with them help me to know myself better. When I'm doing unstructured imagery, any one of them may pop up at any moment.

My Child is a frequent visitor. Since I have begun to pay more attention to him he seems brighter and more energized.

He loves it when I write because it gives him an opportunity to share fantasies with me. He is wonderfully imaginative today just as he was when he acted out story after story with the help of his toy soldiers. Perhaps we shall one day collaborate on a work of fiction.

My Angry Self is the least pleasant of my associates but I've come to understand and appreciate him more. He's really pretty mean and terribly critical.

He tends to feel that he's had a rough life and has coped unwhimperingly with adversity. He's inclined to be contemptuous of those who engage in self pity.

I point out to him that his hostility toward those who are needy and dependent is a means of denying his own dependency and his disappointment in not being as nurtuerd as he would have liked. He won't let down his defenses enough to acknowledge that.

Sir Angry reminds me, and rightly so, that I'd better hang on to him because I'm inclined to be too nice. He is skilled in the art of sarcasm and a brilliant practitioner of the put-down. He is especially good at deflating pompous egos.

Multiple Personality Disorder

Inevitably, the question arises: does this mean we are all multiple personalities like Sybil? The answer is "no" but we need to recognize that we are not all that dissimilar from individuals suffering from Multiple Personality Disorder.

All of us embody, separate from the mainstream character-istics by which we identify ourselves. clusters of feelings, attitudes and behaviors which maintain some degree of independent iden-tity. We have integrated them sufficiently to prevent their taking over or doing as they please on a broad scale but we may recognize their influence on some of our actions and attitudes.

The more intensely we try to control these sub-selves or to eliminate them completely, the more autnonmous they become. By imaging them we acknowledge them as distinct entities worthy of our attention and respect. Paradoxically this leads to integration and greater control over them.

It doesn't matter much whether we image them in the form of a person animal or object. The image is energized by the ego state, no matter what.

The person afflicted with Multiple Personality Disorder has ego states that are not integrated at all and over which she has no control. The various personalities tend to take over executive control and to direct the individual's behavior for indefinite periods until another ego state assumes command. Frequently the personality currently in charge is amnesic regarding what some or all of the others have been doing and may not even know of their existence.

The majority of Multiple Personality Disorder sufferers endured exquisite physical and/or sexual abuse during childhood. As a survival mechanism, sub-selves were given autonomy by the executive in order to relieve it of some of its unbearable stress and prevent its possible anihilation.

Though the person may be delivered from the destructive environment later in life his or her personality, like Humpty Dumpty, cannot be put together again. Shifts from one personality to another continue to occur spontaneously and are often accompanied by drmatic changes in appearance and behavior.

The clinical manifestations of Multiple Personality Disorder are easily distinguished from the imagery experience. Imagery neither induces nor reflects this disorder. However, knowing this does not necessarily dispel some persons' anxiety connected with imaging.

When people first work with imagery, one of the frequent comments is, "That was weird!" or "I felt really crazy doing that!" As we have noted, imagery work promotes something akin to a psychotic experience. This is why it is not generally recommended for someone already in a psychotic state.

Those who are not psychotic seem to have little difficulty recognizing that their images are projections from within themselves. No matter how vivid and gripping the imagery is, they are able to maintain that awareness.

In contrast, psychotic individuals are convinced that their images are real entities located in the outer environment. This issue of locus provides the major distinction between an hallucination and an image.

A Mad Tea Party

The average person on the street looking in on an imagery based psychotherapy session would very likely perceive the observable behaviors as inappropriate, bizarre or insane. The client may be deeply involved in conversation with an invisible animal whom he addresses by name. The therapist may be exhorting the client to carry out some action in regard to this unseen entity and saying encouraging things as the action is carried out, though the action is unobservable.

Gone is the dignity of the stately analyst awaiting the free associations of his couch-bound patient. Gone is the logic of the questions and answers of traditional therapy. Gone is the dictum: be realistic. Is this psychological treatment or a Mad Tea Party?

You may recall the Mad Tea Party from Lewis Carroll's *Alice in Wonderland*. It was an event epitomizing the suspension of the laws of logic and social organization, a prominent characteristic of Wonderland. Just prior to her participation in the tea party, she and the Cheshire Cat had a discussion about madness which went like this:

> "In that direction," the Cat said, waving its right paw round, "lives a Hatter; and in that direction," waving the other paw, "lives a March Hare. Visit either you like; they're both mad."
>
> "But I don't want to go among mad people," Alice remarked.
>
> "Oh, you can't help that," said the Cat; "we're all mad here. I'm mad. You're mad."
>
> "How do you know I"m mad?" said Alice.
>
> "You must be," said the Cat, "or you wouldn't have come here."

When Alice followed the white rabbit down into the rabbit hole she began a journey very much like the shaman's journey into the underworld. In the underworld the shaman talks to animals, encounters benevolent and dangerous spirits and performs such superhuman tasks as flying or changing size.

The shaman, like Alice, has entered a realm where the law and order of the material universe are completely negated. If we equate sanity with rational, sequential thinking and belief that reality is a solid, measurable mass of thing-ness, then we might identify the experiences of both the shaman and Alice as insanity.

The Cheshire Cat hits the nail on the head. Simply by virtue of entering into that realm, Alice earns the label of being mad. When we do imagery work we too have entered the underworld and our actions are similar to those of a mad person.

The shaman is willing to risk experiencing madness because he knows madness cloaks wisdom and healing power. The trick, for him and us is to enter madness and return from it rather than to remain a prisoner inside its borders. The psychotic person has wandered into the Kingdom of Madness and lost her way back.

Are we saying that a little madness can be a good thing? Yes.

Distinguishing Madness from Sanity

Remember that the definition of madness changes from culture to culture and age to age. In his fascinating book, *The Origin of Consciousness in the Breakdown of the Bicameral Mind*, Julian Jaynes (1976) reminds us that Plato called insanity "a divine gift." Jaynes major premise is that human beings have not always had what we call today self awareness, a fairly recent development on the evolutionary time scale. Before self awareness, there was no distinction made between projections from within and events occurring outside of the mind/body system.

What we call thoughts, humans at an earlier stage of development perceived as voices and interpreted them as coming from a supernatural origin. In other words, the basic thinking/feeling processes of these people were what we would now identify as psychotic process.

Following Jaynes' thesis, there was a time in our collective history when, in effect, we were all mad. As a result of that common experience, the root of madness is buried deep within everyone.

We achieve and practice varying degrees of control over it but it is ever there. We sense it. Our fear is that, if we confront it, we shall be engulfed in it forever—that we shall literally lose our minds.

This fear is based on rigid ideas about sanity that are presented to us from the time we are very young. We learned early in life that to be crazy is to lose one's status as a person.

Part of our definition of crazy is based on behaviors and attitudes which were deemed annoying, frightening or otherwise unacceptable by our parents. We learned to equate sane behavior with following the idiosyncratic rules for deportment laid down within the boundaries of our family.

We learned to defend the familial rules by taking the position that o.k.ness is the way us Joneses think, feel and act. Of course, we're doing things right. Those others out there who do things differently are wrong or stupid or insane or all three. We feel safer with people who think and act like we do but both we and they have our little secrets.

For example, disconcerting as it may be to recognize it, all of us "normal" folk spontaneously hallucinate at times. Who among us has never "seen" something which wasn't there? Who among us has not heard our name "called" when no one was around? Who has never detected an odor when others sharing our space smelled nothing?

It is worth stressing, however, that hallucination is not, as many people suppose, a mark of
insanity. ('I must be going bonkers, I'm beginning
to see things that aren't there.') It is practically a
normal occurrence. It is only when reality-testing
fails that a pathological condition may be present;
and even then the cause may be chemical and the
disturbance temporary. (Taylor, 1979)

In a now famous experiment by Rosenhan (1973), eight
sane people secretly gained admission to twelve different hospitals
in five different states. Each pseudopatient stated that he or she
had been hearing voices but simulated no other symptoms upon
admission to the psychiatric ward.

Eleven of the admitting hospitals labeled the pseudopatients
"schizophrenic" and one came up with the diagnosis "manic-
depressive." There is no evidence that physicians or staff on any
of the units recognized these persons as sane.

Rosenhan's study raises serious questions regarding our
ability to identify sanity or insanity. Yet, once the label of insanity
is applied, it tends to stick, no matter what. Under ordinary
circumstances, the subjects in Rosenhan's experiment might
have had to bear undeservingly the schizophrenic stigma for the
rest of their lives. Who can say that many others haven't had to do
just that?

No wonder we are afraid to journey into the dangerously
exciting underworld of Alice and the shaman. Even if we return
intact, we may, like Alice, be labeled mad simply for having been
there.

In spite of the risks, many who have sojourned to the
shadow world have opted to go back again and again. They find the
perilous trip worthwhile. They find there the "something more"
which they have long sensed exists beyond the confines of space,
time, energy and matter.

Throughout history mankind has sought to discover that
"something more." Modern man is no exception.

Walt Disney understood this facet of human nature quite
well. Recognizing that adults as much as children want to keep up
an ongoing romance with the non-material universe, he wisely
named his theme park The Magic Kingdom. Millions have passed
and will continue to pass through its gates.

Imagery is our window onto the realm of magic. Science
says belief in magic is irrational—insane, in the extreme. Our
explorations put us at risk for censure, but there are rewards. One

of my favorite authors, Sheldon Kopp (1982), explains better than
anyone those difficult to articulate rewards.

> "Tolerance for some craziness can be re-
> warding. Irrational thoughts may contain unrec-
> ognized creative inspirations. Unfettered imaginings
> can bring vivid color to an otherwise drab, sensibly
> ordered world. Single-minded sanity soon becomes
> smug complacency. Insistence on always being
> realistic and reasonable makes life dull, emptying
> it of antic fun and wild adventure.
> "Geting beyond ordinary everyday hum-
> drum sometimes requires the *voluntary* suspen-
> sion of that disbelieving critical judgment that we
> usually call 'sanity.' The altered state of conscious-
> ness needed for enriching our experience may
> depend on willingly going mad from time to time."

All of wisdom is not embodied in logical, linear thought.
Scientific knowledge is only one kind of knowledge. It has limitations just like all other methods of investigation.

Primitive people and ancients revered madness because
they believed mad people were in touch with supernatural agents
and, therefore, privy to knowledge the rest of us don't have. In the
state of madness, reality becomes whatever one believes. Mad or
not, beliefs have the power to affect individuals and their environ-
ments in many different ways.

The Case of the Long Black Car

Gilda believed that there were forces in the universe which
did not want her to live. When she was a toddler, her severely
depressed mother on several occasions pressed a pillow into her
face to quiet her down. With her breathing thus cut off, the child
thought that her mother was trying to kill her. Perhaps she was.

These incidents so traumatized Gilda that she became
convinced she had no right to be alive. It seemed obvious to her
that, if she had been so obnoxious a child that her own mother had
seen fit to get rid of her, she must have been a "bad seed," evil and
unlovable.

Through her childhood and adolescence this client was
extremely accident prone and had a few injuries which were life
threatening. At age sixteen, facing surgery for a serious hip
problem, she prayed to die while under the knife. Some time later,
when UFO sightings were in the headlines, she sent out thought

waves to the aliens telling them they could have her to experiment upon or to kill.

When I met Gilda, she was a young mother with a year old child. Her sense of parental responsibility had led her to face her self destructive tendencies. She was afraid she might deliberately involve herself in a car wreck or invite illness by neglecting self care. She feared that, unless she got therapy, she would find some way to be dead. A part of her did not want to inflict this injustice on her child.

Gilda was afraid of imagery. She did not want to encounter her self destructive aspect. I told her that I wanted her to meet a wise and constructive part of herself, her Inner Guide, who could help her deal with the destructive part. She said that talking about all of these sub-selves made her feel "crazy" and she thought the imagery might push her over the edge.

It took a lot of support and encouragement just to get her to visit her special place which turned out to be a tiny cottage on the beach. She sat in a rocker on the porch of the cottage to await the arrival of her Guide.

After a wait of approximately one minute, she said despairingly, "This is going to leave me either crazy or dead."

"What makes you say that?" I inquired, alarmed.

Her face twitched as she spoke. "I hear a roaring sound and it's getting closer. I don't know what it is but it's terrifying."

"Maybe it's somehow connected with your Guide," I suggested.

Gilda shook her head. "No. This is something evil."

I could see her eyes moving beneath the lids. "What are you in touch with?" I asked.

"I see the source of the sound. It's a long, black car coming down the beach. The motor is particularly loud." She raised her hands to cover her ears. "It's stopping right in front."

The patient was visibly growing more anxious by the moment. "Keep describing what's happening," I urged.

"The car is stopped and two men dressed in black are getting out. There's a woman seated inside but I can't see her. The men are smiling and saying my name soothingly. 'Now Gilda. It's all right Gilda.'

"They're coming toward me and I'm afraid of them. They mean to hurt me. Oh, my God!"

My own anxiety level was rising rapidly. "What is it?"

"The car," she said. "Oh, my God. It's a hearse!"

"Gilda," I said, my voice suddenly tense, " get up and run. Don't let the men take you."

The woman's body tensed and her facial expression was anguished. "I can't," she said breathlessly, "I'm petrified."

"O.k., Gilda. I want to be there with you. I want you to see me there. I'm going to help you fight them off. Do you see me?"

A faint smile crossed her face. "I see you running up the beach. You're calling me."

"Good! I'm really there, Gilda. Together we can fight these guys off. I've found an oar on the beach and I'm coming in swinging."

"They've got hold of me and they're dragging me off the porch. They see you coming and one of them lets go to fight with you. I'm kicking and scratching at the other."

I could feel my pulse racing. "Fight him, Gilda! You can fight him."

"I really can, can't I?" she said with surprise. "The woman in the hearse wants me dead but I don't have to give into her."

"Right! I'm swinging that oar. Fight along with me."

"Wow!" she exclaimed, "someone else is helping me out, too. He's real handsome—wears a Greek sailor's hat. He's very strong. The two men are running back to the car. We've got them beat."

When Gilda returned to ordinary consciousness, we both felt tired but victorious. The experience seemed totally real to both of us.

"I told you I was going to go crazy," she said with a laugh.

"That craziness," I said, "allowed you to encounter the very real demons that want to keep you from any life supporting activity. They didn't want you to meet your Guide."

After the melee, Gilda had learned that the young man who came to her rescue was Demetrious, her Guide. He confirmed that the others were Angels of Death and that their victory would have spelled her doom. He and Gilda agreed to join forces in working out a strategy for eliminating them from her life.

Had you looked in on that scene, you would have seen Gilda and me, obviously excited, flailing around, talking to empty space. We were in the underworld. We were having a Mad Tea Party.

Both of us will swear to you that what happened there was completely real in its impact on our minds and bodies. Most importantly, we will swear to you that it strongly promoted Gilda's healing.

Imagery as a Spiritual Connection

Most of the great fictional private eyes are at least eccentric. Conan Doyle's characterization of Sherlock incorporates a distinct touch of madness. It is this very madness which seems to impart to him his superior abilities.

Perhaps the greatest imagist of literature is Cervantes' (1937) *Don Quixote*. His unforgettable feat of imagery was visualizing a windmill as a dangerous dragon and doing battle with it.

Most everyone the Man of LaMancha encountered during his wanderings thought him quite mad. Yet, there was gentleness, humor and lovingness in his insanity. His was a fine madness.

We who image follow in his footsteps. We who talk to animals, gods and demons—who defy the laws of earthly physics - who travel through time and explore surreal landscapes; we who hold moonlight in our hands must remember and respect that others may not see any of that happening. To them, our tales are the ravings of madness and to that charge we can offer no convincing defense.

On second thought, there may be one defense. There are some who aver that imagery is divinely inspired.

They point to the fact that sacred writings and religious tenets of diverse cultures existing in widely separated historical epochs have been based on the visionary experiences of individuals regarded as holy. By and large, these are people who convinced others that they directly communicated with a Higher Power and / or that Higher Power's emissaries.

As previously noted, it is probable that in mankind's infancy the entire universe was looked upon as a sacred place. Gods and spirits were believed to be everywhere and were frequently "seen." There was no notion of a separation between inner experience and what we now call outer reality. In early history, those two dimensions were one and the same.

Through time and with the development of greater technological skills, human beings began to feel more and more separate from Nature and the gods of Nature. Man became the master of those gods.

Gradually, the gulf between man and his gods increased and contact with them became the work of a specialized group, giving rise to the shamanic and priestly castes. Among these specialists, imaging remained the royal road to the realm of the sacred but it did not continue to be the daily practice of the rank and file. The shamans and priests became the intermediaries of the populous in its dealings with unearthly spirits.

The tradition of experiencing God through prayer, meditation and imagery remained strong throughout the Eastern world. These practices became less common in the Judeo-Christian world but were preserved by a solid core of mystics of both faiths. Those who practiced this tradition most fervently were often designated to be saints, prophets or holy ones.

Psychologically, we have been through three major developments:

> 1. In the first stage we were unable to distinguish between the manifestations of our conscious and unconscious minds.
> 2. Next, we evolved consciousness and became neglectful of the unconscious.
> 3. In modern times, with special thanks to Freud, we rediscovered the unconscious and our hidden inner world became a validated reality, separate from our conscious experience.

Perhaps those people we called mystics were aware of and in contact with the unconscious, maintaining a conviction that its teachings were valuable, even when the mainstream of humanity was paying little attention to it. Aside from this, they may have been mostly ordinary people. If so, the example they have set suggests that, if we are fearless enough, each of us has the capacity for mystical experience.

Images of the Holy Ones

Buddha, Mohammed, Jesus and other great religious leaders had remarkable confrontations with images which were recorded and passed on in sacred texts. Many of their followers, like St. Paul in the case of Jesus, encountered religious imagery which totally changed their lives.

All imagery, including that of those identified as holy, emanates from the unconscious and enters awareness by courtesy of the nervous system. This is the basic process by which the most spiritually significant as well as the most mundane of images is accessed.

This does not necessarily preclude a divine origin but it does say that, if a divine force is at work, it is utilizing human neurophysiology as the vehicle of communication. Perhaps this is why we are so often confused when we attempt to distinguish sacred revelation from psychotic experience. In many instances they don't look much different to an observer.

Saint Catherine of Siena, who began having visions when she was six years old, provides us with a case in point. She professed to have entered into a mystical espousal with Christ who presented her with a golden ring bearing precious stones and a blazing diamond in the center. Catherine acknowledged that she wore it always and viewed it frequently. The problem is that she was the only one to whom it was visible.

There seems to be little doubt regarding how this Saint of the Church would fare in a modern psychiatric evaluation. Yet, her holiness was widely attested to and validated for many by the fact that her physical remains have never suffered deterioration since her death (Cruz, 1977).

The images of Saint Teresa of Avila have raised more than one psychological eyebrow by virtue of their content suggesting intense, repressed sexuality. In her most classically Freudian image she is visited by an angel carrying a golden spear with a flame at the tip. He plunges his spear into her heart. The result is that Teresa is left moaning at the sweetness of the pain and feeling on fire with the love of God.

Perhaps, as the ancients believed, madness, or at least some forms of it, can be a divine gift. Perhaps there are elements of psychosis in all religious experiences and mystical elements in all psychoses. Perhaps we must journey through madness before we can stand solidly on sacred ground.

In the Freudian model, the mystical elements of experience are products of a biologically rooted personal unconscious expressing our infantile wishes for a loving, omnipotent parent and an indestructible ego. Our material bodies in the material universe constitute Freudian reality and all else is delusion.

The Jungian system, in contrast, allows for a non-material reality. He agreed with Freud's concept of a personal unconscious but went on to postulate that we also have an unconscious which is shared with all of humankind and which encompasses the totality of our collective experience. Its boundaries extend beyond the confines of the physical world.

According to Jung, the basic idea of God or the God archetype emanates from that collective unconscious and reflects our connectedness with the divine from our earliest evolutionary history. From this viewpoint the idea of God and supernatural forces is not strictly a wish fulfilling device, as Freud would contend.

Jung's theory does not take an absolute stand regarding the existence of God but it allows for the existence of God. Furthermore, it teaches that, if God does exist, it is through the workings of our unconscious that we are able to experience him/her.

It follows, then, that the path to Holy Ground winds its way through the realm of inner experience. The journeys of Self discovery and God discovery are one.

The Case of the Holy Voice

Charlotte is a client who set forth on the path of Self discovery in order to sift some sense of personhood out of the ashes of a childhood of incestuous abuse, an adolescence of painful self consciousness and a young adulthood of depression. As she first peeked beyond the wall of defenses she had erected to protect herself from her pain, she was astonished at how much of herself and her experience she had been avoiding. Images of and dialogues with her Inner Child brought it back to her in bits and pieces.

Attempts to explore her inner landscape for signs of life other than her heartsick Child led to encounters with seemingly demented, destructive entities wandering about like aliens in a strange land who had latched onto her during times when she was most weak and vulnerable. They identified themselves as discarnate spirits who, in their confused states at the moment of their liberation, had refused to complete passage to the Spirit World.

Painfully, one by one, these entities were exorcised, by pointing out to them the light which would guide them to the spiritual plane. They and Charlotte found peace at last but, during that process, she fell into despair of ever being o.k.

It was Charlotte's discovery of her Inner Guide which rescued her from the desert of despondency. This discovery enabled her to recognize that a wise, transcendent part of herself had survived the childhood holocaust unscathed.

Her Guide appeared in the form of Abraham, the first patriarch of the Hebrew people, chosen by Yahweh to establish a new nation. He was to lead Charlotte to the establishment of a new life.

Given Charlotte's superficial involvement with religion throughout her life and lack of familiarity with the Bible, Abraham seemed an unlikely Guide but there he was. He played an active role in the extensive healing which followed.

Charlotte's depression abated. She grew physically, emotionally and spiritually stronger.

Her imagery began to be invaded by visualizations of another time and place. Charlotte was there but was known as Miriam. It was the time of Jesus and she was one of his followers. In vivid and dramatic imagery she found herself present at his crucifixion. In the aftermath of this imagery, she felt a strong connectedness with the Christ.

Charlotte started searching for an organized body of religious people with which she could identify. She soon found one and began worshipping with her new family in Christ. In the midst of all this blossoming spirituality, she began hearing a Voice.

The Voice, which spoke in the manner of Christ or God, alarmed the client and it alarmed me. She described it as "different" from the auditory experiences she had come to know and accept as a normal aspect of therapeutic imagery. The source of this one seemed to be external rather than from within.

This phenomenon had to be regarded as an auditory hallucination. Frequently, such experiences are symptoms of mental breakdown but Charlotte, who was severely impaired mentally and emotionally when I first met her, was better than ever.

We carefully monitored the content of the messages she received, looking for bizarre and inappropriate communications. There were none. They centered on themes of Charlotte being God's own and her being called to do some special work in his/her service.

Occasionally, there were messages for others which she did not clearly understand but was directed to pass on. She did and they seemed to have meaning to the recipients.

Bit by bit, Charlotte has been receiving direction from her Voice which apparently is pointing her toward missionary work or some other job within the Church. She has been told that she is undergoing a process of learning and purification prior to taking on her appointed task.

This process seems to be taking a very long time and the road is not smooth. The Voice has not brought her a life of bliss. Some of its predictions have failed to materialize.

Nevertheless, Charlotte has continued to grow. She has become more assertive, more risk taking and reflects increased self esteem. She is serious about her religion, somewhat dogmatic, but not obnoxious.

My position remains that what she hears is a product of the workings of her nervous system and unconscious processes. Following Horowitz's (1983) classification system, her imagery can be called a paranormal hallucination. It does not, in her case, indicate psychosis.

Identifying Holy Ground

Has Charlotte reached Holy Ground? She believes she has. There are those in her environment who are willing to endow her with blessedness or special power because of her hallucinations. There are those who think her pretty strange.

Since these experiences take place on an intimate, deeply personal level of Charlotte's being, they can neither be validated nor invalidated as connections with the divine for *her*. I see potential danger arising whenever she or others embrace her communications as proclamations to be heeded by anyone beside herself. I believe that, if motivated to do so, every individual is capable of developing transcendent connections of his own and need not rely on the connections of others.

Charlotte is having an exceptional but by no means rare experience. Many others have laid claim to similar phenomena and it is inevitably a judgment call as to whether it is an indication of extraordinary spirituality. It would be the better part of wisdom to require that those who lay claim to holiness on the basis of such unusual and, let's face it, attention grabbing experiences should have to present other and more practical evidence of holiness.

There is a story about an old rabbi and a young rabbi discussing holiness. The young rabbi ecstatically proclaims that the holiest man he has ever known is his teacher, Rabbi Javitz.

"There has never been one more holy," the youth proclaims. "The man is so holy that when he prays his feet are lifted off the ground by the power of God!"

"Ah, yes," says the old rabbi, "but how does he treat his dog?"

The old rabbi's wisdom is useful to all of us. We must be careful not to confuse glitz with holiness.

From the Therapist's Notebook: A Ghost in the Night

Is it possible that imagery allows us to make contact with the spirits world? I have had more than one experience which leads me to ponder that question.

The most significant experience concerns my father who, along with my mother, died the same day in an accident. Both were in their seventies but were maintaining a pretty good quality of life so the event seems especially tragic.

I laid my mother to rest with loving thoughts and feelings. Her imperfections imposed no emotional barrier.

With my father it was more difficult. There were unspoken enmities between us. There was on my part resentment unresolved.

Within a year of his death, my conscious awareness was that I had accepted and forgiven him. I wished with all my heart to communicate this to him. I thought of using imagery to do just that.

On two consecutive days I attempted to bring him into my imagery and failed. I could not determine if it was I who was resisting him or he who was resisting me. I feared that the barriers I had left between us were too strong to be toppled.

During the night following my second attempt I had a wonderful dream, eloquent in its simplicity. I was in a shower and, suddenly, my father was there. We showered together, enjoying the steamy warmth and emerging feeling clean and refreshed. That was it.

There was nothing sexual about the dream but it conveyed a powerful feeling of intimacy. There we were together with our armor and defenses stripped off. We were in communion, being cleansed and renewed.

The next day I invited him into my imagery and he readily appeared. We approached and embraced warmly, then slowly parted. Both of us were at peace.

Imagery and the Occult

For some the connotations of imagery are spiritual but for others it suggests magic and sorcery, even Satanism. There are those who are attracted to imagery primarily because of its occult qualities. It cannot be denied that going into trances, seeing visions and conversing with unseen entities have been traditional staples of such folk as witches, wizards, soothsayers, spiritualists, shamans, prophets, mystics, channelers, mind readers, etc.

Although much of what was formerly referred to as "occult" is now called "parapsychological," the public understanding and acceptance of the practices involved remains limited. You can find people today who still consider such matters to be the work of the Devil.

The attempt to approach paranormal phenomena scientifically has been hampered by the belief of many scientists that it is not a fit subject for science in the first place. Thanks largely to the pioneering efforts of J.B. Rhine (1947), parapsychology has established a niche in the broader field of psychology and, in terms of research and publications, seems to be alive and well.

The parapsychological events being most widely studied are called extrasensory perception (ESP) which refers to the awarness of an event that has not been perceived through the normal sensory apparatus. Specific attention is being paid to mental telepathy, the transmission of thoughts between persons; clairvoyance, knowledge of an object or event not occurring within the range of one's sensory perceptual awareness; psychokinesis, the ability to mentally influence material things; and precognition, knowledge of future events.

Imagery may play a role in any or all of these psychic events. For example, telepathists often report that they receive people's thoughts in the form of pictures and clairvoyants talk of "seeing" that which is not within their visual field.

There is some agreement that all parapsychological events occur within an altered state of consciousness and that persons who are good visualizers demonstrate more parapsychological abilities than those who are not. If these hypotheses are borne out, it becomes easy to understand the long association between imagery and these phenomena because the conditions for both are identical.

The question remaining unresolved is: From whence comes the imagery in parapsychological events? We can stay somewhat within the good graces of most scientists as long as we look upon our images as expressions, distortions or elaborations of our stored up sensory impressions but parapsychology points to the possibility that some of our images may be a kind of seeing beyond the limits of time, space and our own perceptual physiology as we know it.

To make matters more complicated, parapsychological phenomena imply that the images in our mind have the power to directly affect objects and events in our external environment, as when thoughts are sent telepathically to another. These are the pivotal issues upon which some scientists and laymen alike begin to label imagery as nonsense, at best.

These are issues on which one can only speak for one's self. I believe that, eventually, a satisfactory scientific explanation for the things we have been discussing will be found. Like all scientific explanations, it will tell us the mechanics of the phenomena; it will tell us how these things happen. The explanation may be largely based in biology, chemistry, physics or psychology or a combination. Who knows?

However, the scientific explanation will have its limitations as always. Science is not equipped to deal with that which is unquantifiable and unobservable. It may never tell us exactly what an image is.

Perhaps recognition of this gap will lead to the birth of a new branch of science. There are encouraging signs of this in the development of respectable organizations like the Institute of Noetic Sciences which attempts to apply the principles of scientific research to subjects once considered to be strictly metaphysical. There seems to be a growing number of scientists who are, at least, open minded about the non-material universe.

The so-called New Age Movement has brought back into popular awareness ancient healing methods, the power of magic, the importance of myths and human spirituality. Like all movements, it has its kooky fringe but there are many who are caught up in it because they are honestly searching for answers which neither science nor religion in our technological age has supplied.

The Shadow side of the New Age Movement is reflected in the irrational, quick fix sort of spirituality which some of its adherents manifest. They flit from crystals to the Tarot to pyramids to what-have-you as if their ungrounded sampling of a smorgasbord of otherworldly delights will elevate them to the status of a mystic.

From a balanced perspective traditional orthodoxy has its Shadow side too. New Age may generate a certain amount of lunacy and irresponsibility but, at its edge, dogmatic conservatism nurtures its own psychological and political evils in the form of paranoia and fascism.

No matter when or if a satisfactory explanation of it comes along, imagery is and will continue to be a tool for transcending the ordinary boundaries imposed on us by the physical universe. It is one of those rare phenomenon which has established a place of some significance in both science and religion.

Imagery can lift us out of our bodies and out of our world. It allows us to communicate without the confounding medium of words. It is our passport to the realm of the Eternal Now where all time (past, present, future) is one.

The power of imagery is such that it has been identified with magic (white and black), religious experience, insanity and healing medicine. All of this attests to its recognized mystery and potency.

Many of those most concerned about imagery's connection with the occult cite the potential for its use in destructive ways. It is an inescapable fact that any force capable of healing is capable of harming. This does not make imagery a tool of the Devil any more than a curative drug which, deliberately or unintentionally, can be administered in such a way as to bring about the worsening of an illness or death.

I remain open minded regarding the ultimate source of imagery beyond our nervous systems. It may well be our window to another world of experience which does not comply with the laws of the physical universe.

One of the characters in *The Brothers Karamazov* (*Dostoevsky*, 1949) is the monk, Father Zosima. Among his exhortations, we find the following:

> Much on earth is hidden from us, but to make up for that we have been given a precious sense of our living bond with the other world, with

the higher heavenly world, and the roots of our thoughts and feelings are not here but in other worlds. That is why the philosophers say that we cannot apprehend the essence of things on earth.

God took seeds from other worlds and sowed them on this earth, and planted a garden, and everything came up that could come up, but what He grew lives and is alive only through the feeling of its contact with other mysterious worlds.

CHAPTER SEVENTEEN

WHERE DO THEY GO? WHERE DO WE GO?

My experience of certain images suggests that they are attached to specific places. Some are geographically or historically significant but most are not. In either case, the energy behind the image seems to be rooted in that particular spot.

These power points are one of the wonders of that make travel anywhere such an adventure. The sojourner might well discover one at the very next stop on the itinerary.

I had no idea when we arrived at Mont-Saint-Michel, that magnificent abbey and church belonging half to the land and half to the sea, that it would generate an extraordinarily vivid image. That image is a good example of what we are examining here.

It occurred as we stood in the great hall where pilgrims from many lands had ended their long journeys. How welcome the great fireplace with its warmth and sustenance must have been to them.

At some point as I gazed about, the hall was transformed. I was no longer standing there with twentieth century tourists.

I was somewhere back in time, huddled with fellow pilgrims. The sense of it was utterly real.

Still cold and damp from the road, I was pushing my way toward the burning logs in the fireplace. The air was heavy with the smell of unwashed bodies. I was surrounded by the sounds of humanity: coughing, children crying, whispered words between companions.

When I reached the hearth, a bowl of thin gruel was pressed into my hands. I swallowed from it eagerly. It had not much taste but the warmth of it trickling down my throat was marvelous.

A Benedictine novice was serving the gruel. He and I were young men of about the same age. We smiled at each other.

Someone began intoning prayers in Latin. "Pater noster qui es in coelis......"

Abruptly I was back in the present. I might have thought little of the incident had it not been so vivid.

Mont-Saint-Michel is just one of the special places that has generated exceptional imagery for me. Prominent among others have been Stonehenge, Mt. Fujiyama and Muir Woods.

Some spots close to home have the same effect. There is the pond where in fantasy I first met Arrow. There is the fallen pine tree which survived for many years on its side with most of its roots out of the ground. There are the burial sites of loved ones and, on our ranch, the graves of many of our animals most of which I dug myself. A visit to any of these spots is apt to elicit special imagery.

I can sit at the graveside of a beloved pet, close my eyes and be treated to a visit from its bounding, energetic spirit. Magically these experiences have many times translated themselves into poetry which, as I go inside and write it down, seems as if it is being dictated by an unseen, outside source.

There seems to be a world of images which touches the material world yet exists on its own. It is mostly subtle but at certain times and in certain places it demands our attention.

I think of my images as my friends. They take me to the farthest reaches of my mind and the beginnings of my being. They chronicle as a motion picture might the Myth which is my life. They reveal my body and my mind, my light and my shadow, my perception of the material world and my perception of all possible worlds.

Swedish director, Ingmar Bergman, ends his motion picture, *Persona* (Lopert Pictures Corp., 1966), with a shot of the film in the projector running out and the lamp dying. It is his way of telling the audience that the imagery is over.

This deeply affecting closing scene reminds us that the images will continue to exist on the film that has just run its course. Somewhere that film in a can continues its existence and the images that make up *Persona* have an ongoing life.

Similarly, when I complete an imagery experience, I have a sense of departing from my image or it departing from me. In either case there is an implication that we are going separate ways rather than either of us ceasing to be. I am confident that I can return to it again and again if I wish and I know it has the power to return to me if it wills to do so.

Therefore, I think of images as having their own realm of existence. When I receive images, it is like receiving visitors from another dimension and, when I enter into their domain, it is like crossing over to another plane of being.

Where, exactly, do our images go when we are done with them? How is it that the next time we encounter them they may have evolved in appearance, gained information, or recount new experiences? If they are simply a manifestation of brain activity, why can't the consciously functioning brain do and know the things that they do and know?

I have no definitive answers but it seems to me that our images' point of origin has to be a place free from the constraints of the physical world. It is this freedom from the begrudging bonds of the material universe that infuses them with the power to heal us and help us grow.

In the Realm of Imagery nothing is impossible. There is no such thing as hopelessness.

Imagery flows from the Imagination which by definition is the not-real. Yet, the Imagination itself is subjectively real to each of us and an undeniable "fact" of our lives.

In the Land of Imagination, the Inner Child (the Child we once were and will never cease to be) remains forever a Child. That Child within each of us is the fountainhead of our capacity for loving and being loved.

Having that perennial Child within is a special blessing for those of us who have deep wounds to heal from our childhood. It means we have a lifetime to teach the Child love by loving it.

Likewise, we have the opportunity to work right up until our last day on becoming our Best Self. It is the part of us ever evolving toward greater health and wholeness, ultimately spiritual health and wholeness.

Our Looking Glass Self can tell us where we are with life at any of its stages. By facing it in imagery, we bravely refuse to run from our Shadow side. Through interaction with it, we can keep track of how we are changing and how and when we need to modify our behaviors or attitudes.

Our Inner Guide is also a lifetime companion. He or she will be with us every step of the way on our journey through the universe, providing support, direction and wisdom. The Guide is a comforting presence from which no one can separate us.

Through these companions and other subselves which make us uniquely who we are, we attain power. We have the wherewithal to call forth images of the things we most fear and the things we most cherish. By facing our fears imaginally we can increase strength and courage for confronting them in the material world. Many times, we can modify or eliminate them completely.

Similarly, with imagery, we can face our symptoms as messengers. We can be bold enough to decipher their coded communications and to make healing use of the wisdom embeded therein.

On the wings of color we can allow imagery to carry us to secret places where lost fragments of our lives can be unearthed. Then, we can allow those same colors to transport us to new horizons of growth and development.

If we are willing to watch and learn, the imagery of our language will teach us. The words we know and choose to use are a deeply personal reflection of who we are. Those words can speak to us out of a collective past in which they evolved from deeply felt experience.

And there are our dreams. They are an abundant source of knowledge cloaked in the richness of symbolism. Our dream images beckon to us every night. We have the means to call them forth at any time and to hear what they would have us know.

Without images none of this is possible. Ironically, we can't even explain what an image is or agree on how it is produced. In our materialistic society, it is easy to discount its importance altogether.

No matter how much imagery is discounted, it remains a universal phenomenon. Everyone images.

We continue to image throughout life and, according to researchers such as Kubler-Ross (1978), Osis (1961) and Ring (1984), right up until the moment of death. These authors present a wealth of evidence that many dying or declared dead individuals receive vivid images of previously departed loved ones or archetypal figures in their final moments. Death, rather than a fade-out into darkness, is described as movement into incredible light.

We depart this life with images and possibly begin it with them already enfolded in the depths of our being through our collective unconscious. Is it possible that we being to image during our embryonic life? Most assuredly we do in early infancy.

Throughout life and even unto death the Realm of Imagery beckons us. Our private eyes with their flair for adventure are drawn to its borders. The part of us forged by civilization, materialism and scientism urges us to stay away.

In the final analysis, it is my mystical self which is most enamored of imagery. Through its workings, from time I think I can see the other side and there are wonders there. I respect those who say there really is no other side—that all this fuss is just wishful thinking at best, madness at worst.

But it is a very fine madness.

By experimenting with some or all of the imagery exercises outlined in this book you can begin to formulate your own opinion. I can only tell you that I have seen many people deeply affected by the use of imagery techniques.

The only way to know if this will be true for you is to point yourself toward that other side, let go and see what happens.

> "What matters it how far we go?" his scaly friend replied.
> "There is another shore, you know, upon the other side.
> "The further off from England the nearer is to France—
> "Then turn not pale, beloved snail, but come and join the dance."
>
> —Lewis Carroll
> Alice's Adventures in Wonderland

REFERENCES

Achterberg, Jeanne. *Imagery in Healing: Shamanism and Modern Medicine*. Boston: New Science Library Shambhala, 1985.

Ahsen, Akhter. *Basic Concepts in Eidetic Psychotherapy*. New York: Brandon House, 1973.

Assagioli, Robert. *Psychosynthesis: A Manual of Principles and Techniques*. New York: Viking Press, 1971.

Baum, L. Frank. *The Wizard of Oz*. New York: Grosset & Dunlap: 1963

Berne, Eric. *What Do You Say After You Say Hello?* New York: Grove Press, 1972.

Blair, Lawrence. *Rhythms of Vision*. New York: Schocken Books, 1976.

Bresler, D.E. and Trubo, R. *Free Yourself from Pain*. New York: Simon and Schuster, 1979.

Carroll, Lewis. *The Works of Lewis Carroll*. Guiliano, Edward (ed.). New York: Crown Publishers, 1982.

Castenada, Carlos. *A Separate Reality*. New York: Simon and Schuster, 1971.

Cervantes, Miguel de. *Don Quixote of the Mancha*. Shelton, Thomas (trans.) New York: P.F. Collier and Son, 1937.

Cruz, Joan. *The Incorruptibles*. Rockford, Ill.: Tan Books and Publishers, 1977.

Doyle, Arthur C. *The Annotated Sherlock Holmes*. Baring-Gould, William S. (ed.). 2 vols. New York: Clarkson N. Potter Inc., 1967.

Eliot, T.S. *The Waste Land and Other Poems*. Orlando: Harcourt Brace Jovanovich, 1934.

Epstein, Gerald. *Healing Visualizations: Creating Health Through Imagery*. New York: Bantam Books, 1989.

Erickson, Milton H. *The Collected Papers of Milton Ericksonon on Hypnosis*. Rossi, Ernest (ed.) New York: Irvington, 1980.

Freud, Sigmund. *The Basic Writings of Sigmund Freud*. Brill, A.A. (tr. & ed.). New York: Random House, 1938.

Grof, Stanislav. *The Adventure of Self Discovery*. Albany: SUNY Press, 1988.

Gunther, Bernard. *What To Do Till the Messiah Comes*. New York: The Macmillan Co., 1971.

Harner, Michael. *The Way of the Shaman*. New York: Bantam Books, 1982.

Horowitz, Mardi. *Image Formation and Psychotherapy*. New York: Jason Aronson, Inc., 1983.

Jaffe, Dennis and Bresler, David. "The Use of Guided Imagery as an Adjunct to Medical Diagnosis and Treatment," *Journal of Humanistic Psychology*. Vol. 20, No. 4, 1980.

Jaynes, Julian. *The Origin of Consciousness in the Breakdown of the Bicameral Mind*. Boston: Houghton Mifflin Co., 1976.

Jung, Carl G. *The Basic Writings of C.G. Jung*. De Laszlo, Violet Staub (ed.) New York: Random House, 1959.

Kubler-Ross, Elisabeth. *To Live Until We Say Good-Bye*. Englewood Cliffs, N.J.: Prentice-Hall, 1978.

Lad, Vasant. *Ayurveda: The Science of Self Healing*. Santa Fe, NM: Lotus Press, 1984.

Lazarus, Arnold. *In the Mind's Eye*. New York: Guilford, 1977.

Leuner, Hans C. "Guided Affective Imagery (GAI)," *American Journal of Psychotherapy*. Vol. 23, No. 6, 1969.

Ley, Robert. "Cerebral Laterality and Imagery" in Sheikh, A. (ed.) *Imagery: Current Theory, Research and Application*. New York: Wiley and Sons, 1983.

Moore, Marianne. "The Mind is an Enchanting Thing" in *The Complete Poems of Marianne Moore*. New York: The Macmillan Co. Viking Press, 1967.

Osis, Karlis. *Deathbed Observations by Physicians and Nurses*. New York: Parapsychology Foundation, 1961.

Oyle, Irving. *Time, Space and the Mind*. Millbrae, CA: Celestial Arts, 1976.

Rhine, J.B. *The Reach of the Mind*. New York: William Sloane Associates, 1947.

Ring, Kenneth. *Heading Toward Omega: In Search of the Near-Death Experience*. New York: Morrow, 1984.

Rosenhan, D.L. "On Being Sane in Insane Places." *Science*. Vol. 179, January 1973.

Samuels, Mike and Samuels, Nancy. *Seeing with the Mind's Eye*. New York: Random House, 1975.

Samuels, M. and Bennett, H. *The Well Body Book*. New York: Random House, 1973.

Sheikh, A.A., Twente, G.E. and Turner, D. "Death Imagery: Therapeutic Uses" in Sheikh, A.A. and Shaffer, J.T. (eds.) *The Potential of Fantasy and Imagination*. New York: Brandon House, 1979.

Shorr, E. et al (eds.) *Imagery: Its Many Dimensions and Applications*. New York: Plenum, 1980.

Siegel, Bernie. *Love, Medicine and Miracles*. New York: Harper and Row, 1986.

Simonton, O., Simonton, S. and Creighton, J. *Getting Well Again*. Los Angeles: J.P. Tarcher, 1978.

Stokes, Louis and Stokes, Beverly Carol. "Conception Imagery Exercise: Journey to Beginning" in Sheikh, A.A. (ed.) *Anthology of Imagery Techniques*. Milwaukee: American Imagery Institute, 1986.

Watkins, J. and Watkins, H. "The Theory and Practice of Ego State Therapy," in Grayson, H. (ed.). *Short Term Approaches to Psychotherapy*. New York: National Institute for the Pschotherapies and Human Sciences Press, 1979.

Watson, John B. "Psychology as the Behaviorist Views It," *Psychological Review*, Vol. 20, pp. 158-77, 1913.

Whitman, Walt. *Leaves of Grass*. New York: Doubleday and Co., 1940.

Wilber, Ken. *Up From Eden*. Boulder, CO: Shambhala, 1981.

Wolpe, Joseph. *The Practice of Behavior Therapy*. New York: Pergamon Press, 1969.